a short course in

kindness

a little book on the importance of love
and the relative unimportance
of just about everything else

a short course in

kindness

a little book on the importance of love
and the relative unimportance
of just about everything else

 C_B

Margot Silk Forrest

L. M. Press C_B   Cayucos, California

L. M. PRESS
P.O. Box 345
Cayucos, CA 93430
(805) 545-0888
fax (805) 435-1472
www.AShortCourseinKindness.com

Publisher's Cataloguing-in-Publication Data
Forrest, Margot Silk.
   A short course in kindness : a little book on the importance of
   love and the relative unimportance of just about everything else /
   Margot Silk Forrest. – 1st ed.

   p. cm.
   Includes bibliographical references and index.
   ISBN: 0-9708049-0-3

   1. Kindness.   2. Self-esteem.   3. Self-management (Psychology).
   4. Empathy.   I. Title.

BJ1533.K5F67 2002   177'.7
                           QBI33-589

For my brother, Gil,

a man of great kindness and frequent laughter

1947 - 1986

♧

I have not seen so likely an ambassador of love.

—William Shakespeare

Table of Contents

♋

First Things First:

Some Definitions

Course

An onward movement, progress; a way, path, passage or channel of movement, the direction taken, a natural order or development, flow.

—From *Webster's New World Dictionary*

Kindness

Affection, assistance, benevolence, compassion, generosity, goodness, grace, helpfulness, humanity, loving-kindness, patience, service, tenderness, thoughtfulness, tolerance, understanding.

—From *Chambers Dictionary of Synonyms and Antonyms*

Book

One person's ideas, opinions and stories. To be taken under consideration and weighed against one's own experience. Useful ideas may be adopted, others discarded. Not to be taken as gospel, even if read aloud into a microphone. (Be especially cautious of people with microphones — sometimes it goes to our heads.)

—From the author

ɔჳ

Foreword

by Catherine Ryan Hyde,
author of *Pay It Forward*

The fact that you picked up this wonderful little book in the first place says something encouraging about you. I applaud the place in you that's curious about what it has to offer. It has a great deal to offer. And so, I'm sure, do you. After all, a book can't put something into you that wasn't there to begin with. You bring your own gifts, and a good book like this one helps bring them out into the light.

Since the release of *Pay It Forward*, hundreds of people have told me, each in his or her own unique way, that the book or movie put a voice to something they've tried to do all their lives. Many tell me that passing along spontaneous acts of kindness has been a tradition in their family for years, even generations. I see this as the secret behind the popularity of the Pay It Forward concept. It touches a place in the reader that was there all along. We don't need to learn kindness. Kindness is natural. We need to unlearn the lessons that caused us to ignore our natural impulse in the first place.

I firmly believe that we are born optimistic and altruistic. I used to believe it was pounded out of us at a certain age, that it died in the difficult process of growing up. I don't believe that anymore. I can't. In the last couple of years, I've watched it wake up again in too many people. Now what I believe is this: In the process of growing to adulthood, we make choices about what we'll show others and what we will hide. If it feels too dangerous to put some part of ourselves on display, we put it away where others can't use it to hurt us.

The kindness movement, which I see growing all around me, makes it easier and safer for people to come forward with their own kind impulses. It makes people more likely to find and exercise what I call their "Inner Trevor." A social movement provides safety in numbers. There is no telling how much the world can improve if a sweeping movement of kindness provides a safe platform for change.

Many people tell me they don't know how to get started. They don't have any ideas for kind acts. That seems unimaginable to me. I see need everywhere I go. I tell them the idea is not to sit home and invent kind acts, but to go through life more tuned to the needs of others. When you see a need you can fill, you'll know it.

I have a theory as to how and why we learned to close our eyes to the need and suffering all around us. And it has nothing to do with selfishness or lack of caring.

Take homelessness, an enormous example of human suffering. Most of us, when faced with a homeless person lying on the street, will turn away. I've heard people use this as an example of how cold we've become. I see just the opposite. I see it as a sign that we do care. It instinctively hurts us to see a fellow human in this degraded condition, but — and here is the factor I consider so important — we feel powerless to do anything about it. There is so much homelessness and only one of us. We could struggle all our lives and barely make a dent. So we become discouraged and do nothing at all.

Somehow, then, we have come to believe that changing the world means leaving nothing unchanged, when in reality we need only make a series of positive contributions. Each act of kindness we contribute inspires others. The world begins to change a little at a time. Once we get things going in the right direction, there's no telling how far it could go.

If you're wondering whether it will really work, stop and ask yourself to define what you mean by the word "work." If things get better, did it work? And if you add kindness to the world, won't things get better?

This unique and thoughtful little book will give you all the ideas you need, all the inspiration you can take in. The feeling that you don't know where to begin, or that you want to change the world but don't know how, will evaporate. Yes, a book can do all that. The words we exchange with each other are that powerful.

Within the words you share with others lies your power to change the world. Please use it well.

Introduction

I scarcely know where to begin,
but love is always a safe place.

—EMILY DICKINSON, LETTER TO FANNY AND LOUISE NORCROSS

Nothing teaches us so much about the importance of
kindness as the lack of it. Unkindness — or the
numbing lack of kindness — seems to reach into every
corner of our lives. We have all felt its icy touch:
Someone shoves their cart ahead of ours at the check-out
line, driver after driver stares past us or accelerates when
we try to merge into traffic, or the young woman at the
Returns counter interrupts our explanation of how the
lamp gave our son an electrical shock when he—
"Whatever-r-r," she says under her breath, as she turns

back to her monitor and punches the keys that will get us out of her face.

You could say it's the pressure we're all under that makes us act this way. Too much to do, too little time to do it, too little money, too little joy. But what about the man in the mid-sized Chevrolet who passes me on the highway one morning, then turns, aims his forefinger at me, and pulls the trigger? What provoked *that*? I wonder. Who *am* I to him?

Or the guy driving the battered pickup truck loaded with bags of concrete and displaying a bumper sticker that I have the unhappy opportunity to contemplate while stopped at a traffic light. It reads: I'D SMACK YOU BUT SHIT SPATTERS. I actually shake my head as if this will clear my vision. Surely I must have read the thing wrong.

Another day I'm on a backcountry road, curving down into a dell of craggy live oaks hung with Spanish moss, when a young woman drives past in a blazingly red convertible. Her long hair whips in the wind, and the sticker on her bumper declares: SCREAMING BITCH. As her car disappears around the next curve, I wonder if someone gave her the bumper sticker. Or maybe, I think with unfounded optimism, she doesn't know it's there. The reality is, I admit as I slow for the next tree-lined curve, she probably bought it for herself. Sometimes our acts of unkindness, unconscious or not, are aimed at ourselves.

We all have stories like this — or worse. Their effect is not negligible. We carry them inside us for years.

Someone has reached out and touched us — and it didn't feel good. I may not get the creeps anymore when I think of the well-groomed stranger who "shot" at me in my car, but my attitude toward life is colored by his angry gesture. True, the whole event took only four seconds, but even a single drop of red will tint a can of white paint.♥

We are not immune to each other. We were made to live in community. We are affected by the words and actions of others. When we encounter unkindness, we are diminished — no matter how strong, self-sufficient, and independent we may be.

But it works both ways. Just as we remember for years one act of unkindness, so we will remember an act of kindness: the fellow worker who walked up to a young woman during a pelting ice storm just as she got behind the wheel of her car and said, "I noticed your tires were a little bald. How about if I give you a ride home? I could pick you up in the morning and drive you in."

Or the woman behind the deli counter who secretly made my friend Holly her favorite sandwich and slipped it into her grocery bag one evening as Holly left the market, exhausted but still headed over to the Alzheimer's unit to see her mother and tuck her in for the night. "And *this* on one of those days where people cut me off driving," Holly recalls, "and the millions of other things that happen where you think, 'Life stinks.' What she did was simple. It was tiny. It wasn't a lot of

---

♥ This sad truth was pointed out to me by Marilyn VanDerbur.

money — $3 maybe — but I felt like I'd been given a shot of adrenaline. It *carried* me. I swear the molecules rearranged inside me."♥

You will discover some surprising truths as you read the stories in this book:

- ♥ Kindness brings us into the full use of our personal power.
- ♥ Our ability to give and receive kindness depends on the kindness we hold for ourselves.
- ♥ There is a crucial difference between being nice and being kind: One increases stress, the other reduces it.
- ♥ Kindness is love, pure and simple.
- ♥ One of the shortest paths to self-discovery is the conscious practice of kindness.

Stories are humanity's oldest way of sharing knowledge and wisdom. And few stories are more appealing than those where love wins out. That's the kind of story you will find in this book.

Something about stories like this makes us want to tell them to the people we know. What's more, each time we tell someone a story of love and kindness, it multiplies. That's one of the purposes of this book. It is filled with true stories about kindness. One or more of them will touch you, make you feel good or hopeful or moved, and you will share it with someone else. You

---

♥ All the stories of kindness in this book are true.

might tell the story to a colleague over coffee during a break in your hectic day. You might recount it to your family at dinner one night. You might type it into an email♥ and send it off to a friend. Any way you share it, the story will spread.

And willing ears will hear it. As much as we are drawn to the television or daily paper for its coverage of terrible events, we are drawn even more strongly to reports of events that rebuild our faith in human nature, that "encourage" us — literally put courage into us.

I believe that we — individually and collectively — have huge untapped reserves of kindness. What we need is the motivation to draw upon them more often. Stories are one of the things that can provide that motivation. Why? Because kindness — like fear, apathy, selfishness, and measles — is contagious.

The difference is, it's contagious in a good way.

♥ Along with the name of the book where you read it, I hope.

A SHORT COURSE IN KINDNESS

℅

CHAPTER 1

You Can Catch It in the Best of Company

As we...act with kindness, perhaps, or with
indifference or hostility toward the people we
meet, we are setting the great spider web
atremble. The life I touch for good or ill will
touch another life, and that in turn another,
until who knows where the trembling stops or
in what far place my touch will be felt.

—FREDERICK BUECHNER, QUOTED IN *SPIRITUAL LITERACY*

It's August in Chicago and it's hot. Really hot. And
muggy to boot. The city bus Tovah is riding to work is
crowded, just like it is every morning rush hour. She
hates it. She's black and she's a teenager and she's treated

like a nobody on this bus. She's feeling sweaty and mean. There's no way she's giving up her seat, not to anyone. Things are bad enough without riding the bus standing up and getting pushed around. Who cares what people think? She's staying put.

Then a man shouts, "Hey, guess what this gorilla did?" It's a white guy and he's holding a newspaper. He starts reading it aloud in a booming voice. " 'A toddler who fell into a gorilla exhibit at the Brookfield Zoo on Friday afternoon was rescued by a female gorilla who cradled the child and brought him to zookeepers.' It says she saved him from six other gorillas!"

"All of a sudden people are smiling and talking to each other, almost like friends," Tovah recalls. "I never saw that on a bus." Then someone asks the man to read the story again, and other people open their papers and start reading it, and pretty soon the whole bus is excited about what the gorilla did. "Everybody is talking about the same thing and looking straight at each other...We're so *happy*.

"Then guess what I did? I got up and gave my seat to an old lady. I just up and did it," Tovah says in wonder. "Without hardly knowing I was going to...I wanted to do something good too."♥

❦

♥ I discovered Tovah's story in Vivian Gussin Paley's gem of a book, *The Kindness of Children*.

Amazing, isn't it? Not only is kindness contagious, it is *so* contagious that we can catch it from a gorilla. Why is that? Why did the people on the bus start smiling at each other? It's not like *they* saved the child. And why did they start looking "straight at each other"?

These may sound like rhetorical questions, but they're not. Let's conduct a little inquiry. We might discover something interesting here.

First, it seems safe to say that the people on the bus were smiling and laughing because they were happy. But *why* were they happy? They didn't know the little boy who was saved. They didn't know his parents. Maybe they were just glad that he was rescued before anything worse happened to him. That makes sense. But what about this: Would they have felt as happy if the child had been saved by keepers rushing in with sticks to keep the gorillas at bay while they grabbed the boy? What do you think? Run that scenario through your mind and see how it makes you feel.

Here's what I noticed going on in my mind when I played the zookeeper-rescue scenario. First my feelings went from neutral (I'm riding a bus) to fearful (I hear that a child fell into a pit filled with gorillas). Then, when I pretend to myself that zookeepers rescued the boy, my fear subsides and my feelings go back to neutral (nothing terrible happened, wonder if I'll get to work on time). I'm relieved, but I'm not moved to happiness.

Let's set that aspect of the situation aside for a moment and look at the second amazing thing that happened on the bus (aside from Tovah's revolutionary act of kindness): People looked into each others' faces. They no longer kept their eyes riveted on their paperbacks or newspapers or the ribbed hard-rubber floor or the strip ads above the grimy windows. They stopped pretending they were the only ones on the bus. They stopped worrying about what they might see in their neighbor's face — rage or misery or madness or whatever it was they had been on guard against. They stopped keeping their emotional distance in case the stranger whose shoulders or hips were pressed against theirs might want something from them.

This tells me that the people on the bus not only felt happy themselves after hearing the gorilla story, they knew that their fellow riders would be happy too. They didn't assume this, they *knew* it. They didn't peek at each other first to be sure it was safe to let their guard down. They just did it. They took the irrevocable and usually risky step of looking straight into the eyes of a stranger — and smiling!

So there was suddenly a deep feeling of community — as well as genuine happiness — on that sweltering bus packed with people rumbling its way into downtown Chicago on an August morning in 1996. Looked at that way, it sounds like a miracle must have occurred. It certainly did for Tovah, who found herself surprised by her own joy.

"Surprised by joy." That's the phrase C.S. Lewis used to describe what he felt when he finally awoke to the immensity of God's love for him and for all of creation. He interpreted what he experienced through the filter of his religion, Christianity, so to him it was "God's love." But I think Tovah and C.S. Lewis and everyone on that crowded bus experienced the same thing, whether they were Christians, Hindus, Buddhists, Jews, or non-believers: They were given a compelling piece of evidence for the benevolent nature of the universe.

The people hearing about the gorilla were laughing and smiling because something truly *good* had happened. Something totally unexpected. It was like a little gift from the universe, a reminder that we are not alone out here on our spinning chunk of rock. We have not been left to sink or swim. We have each other and we have Spirit — whatever name we choose to give it.

That message went straight into the hearts of the people on that bus, unmediated by the rational mind, which would have wanted to question and analyze the experience, that being its job. Everyone who heard the gorilla story that morning *knew* — without even knowing they knew — that everyone else's heart had been touched too.

But our inquiring minds now want to ask, How did they know this? Was it part of the message? If there is benevolence at the core of the universe, does this mean there is benevolence at the core of each of us? Maybe so. It's certainly a question that has been argued for centuries.

I think the answer lies in this essential fact about the nature of life: We are all interconnected in ways deeper and broader that we have ever imagined. At the beginning of this chapter, Protestant minister and writer Frederick Buechner talks about the spider web that trembles when any one of us acts, sending shivers to every part of the web.

There is a famous metaphor in both Buddhist and Hindu mythology that captures this notion of the universe as a web of being. Indra's Net is like an infinite silken fishing net stretching across time and space. A pearl sits at each intersection of its crisscrossing threads. And each pearl reflects the image of every other pearl in the net. In just this way does each of us receive and reflect back to others the light of everyone we come into contact with. No wonder kindness is contagious.

In fact, our actions are contagious no matter what their nature. Whether we join together in laughter or in ridicule, we are setting the web atremble. We are irrevocably interconnected, for better or worse. Like a grove of aspens, all seemingly separate trees but in reality united beneath the soil, we are a members of a single family. The family of man.

СЗ

CHAPTER 2

We Are Kin

We are all tied together in a single garment
of destiny, an inescapable network of mutuality.

—DR. MARTIN LUTHER KING

A young white woman is sitting in her little red car in a multistory parking garage. Her body is shaking. Her forehead is resting on her hands, which are clutching the steering wheel at twelve o'clock. Tears stream down her flushed face as she struggles for breath between sobs. She is feeling lonely and helpless and unloved. A soft rapping at her car window makes her turn her head. A middle-aged black woman is leaning over, looking in.

"Ma'am," she says. "It gets better. I promise."

CS

When I began to think about writing this book, I decided to look up the root of the word kindness. Often the origins of a word can illuminate a deeper meaning that has been outpaced by time.

"Kindness" has the same root as the word kind, of course, and "kind" comes from the Middle English word *kynd*, which comes from the Old English word *cynd*. The latter, says Webster's in a rare moment of wordplay, is "akin to" the German word *Kind*, meaning child.

Hmm. Does kindness mean treating everyone as if they were a child? Seems odd. Then the light dawns. Not "a child," but "our child." Our *Kind*, our kin. Treat everyone as kin. As family. As blood relatives. Which, in fact, we are.

When I was five, a slim book of photographs appeared on the coffee table in our living room. I might not have noticed it except for the fact that this particular coffee table was a favorite hangout of mine. It consisted of a giant circular tray of bronze resting on carved legs inlaid with ivory. The generous one-inch lip around the tray's rim made it the perfect track for racing my marbles. Zing, zing, zing, around they went, faster and faster and faster! ZING, ZING, ZING! I marvel my mother didn't trade it in for a more restful piece of furniture.

Between marble races one day, I reach over and flip open the book of photographs. They are like the snapshots my father takes, all black and white. The first picture is of a naked lady lying on her tummy on a carpet of soft leafy plants covering a forest floor. Her bottom looks very white against the dark leaves of the plants all around her. She has her hair pinned up, like my mother does sometimes, and her eyes are closed. I turn the page and see a picture of a big room that has photographs hung all over its walls. There's also a little picture of a man wearing glasses with round frames. Much later, when I am old enough to care, I will learn he is the renowned photographer Edward Steichen, and the pictures are ones he selected for an exhibit at the Museum of Modern Art in New York in 1955. It was called "The Family of Man."

But at five, I don't know any of that. All I know is the photographs I see and the words my mother will read me from the front of the book: "The first cry of a newborn baby in Chicago or Zamboango, in Amsterdam or Rangoon, has the same pitch and key, each saying, 'I am! I have come through! I belong! I am a member of the Family.' "♥ I like hearing those words a lot. They make me feel good. Like *I* belong, too.

When my sticky little-girl fingers turn the pages of this book, I see people kissing: black people and white people, old people and young people, rich people and poor people. I see people getting married in kimonos, in long white dresses, in what my mother tells me are saris. There are girls playing dress-up in England and a boy

---

♥ From Carl Sandburg's prologue to *The Family of Man*.

learning a special dance in Java. There are kids fighting, crying, laughing, and being held. There are whole families posing proudly for the camera outside their straw hut on the dusty plains of Africa and by the black pot-bellied stove in their living room. There are people working, praying, making music, learning to write the alphabet, gambling, voting, dying, begging for food.

The lesson those photographs taught — a gutsy lesson, indeed, in those xenophobic, Russki-fearing days of the Cold War — became so much a part of me, I never knew it was a lesson I had learned. It was simply how I saw the world. Everyone is just like me; I am just like everyone else. We all have families and lovers and babies and fights. We all cry and make up. All colors, all shapes of eyes and bodies, all faiths, all temperaments, all, all, all.

Where did we ever get the idea that we are different from each other? Because "they" have a different color skin? Because "they" have a different name for god — or no name for god? Because "they" wear cloth wrapped around their heads? Because "their" noses are bigger or smaller or shaped differently? We should try explaining that to a visitor from outer space — and admit while we're at it that these huge differences are reasons we shun or hate or kill each other. The alien would look at us suspiciously, one eyebrow raised over the first of her six striped eyes, and climb promptly back into her spaceship. So much for intergalactic friendship.

The truth is, *nobody* is "them." "They" are just like "us." They want to be happy. They want their children to be happy. They want to be safe and healthy and appreciated. What's more, there are no strangers either; there are no outsiders. We are all insiders. Every person we see, from the CEO of a corrupt corporation to the teacher who told our ten-year-old son he was stupid to the bag lady slumped on the sidewalk in the Bowery, is someone's son or daughter, just as we are. I do not have to like any of these people, but I cannot deny our ultimate kinship.

Can I look at other people — no matter their values or appearance — and think, *Son, daughter, brother. Sister, mother, father. Grandmother, cousin, nephew. Niece. Kin. You and I are kin. We belong to the same family, we breathe the same air. Our hearts beat in the same dance of contraction and release. We stare at the same stars in the black dome of the night sky.*

If I could think this way, would I ever walk past a homeless person with a *moue* of embarrassment or annoyance at being confronted with their needs, at having to smell their unwashed bodies? How could I? I know I cannot change the life of every homeless person I encounter — or *any* homeless person I encounter — but I can give them the gift of contact. I can recognize our shared humanity by looking into their eyes without judgment or disgust. I can notice all we have in common: mouth, fingers, hair, breath, the capacity for pain. I can say "Good luck" or "Bless you" if I am moved to. I can give money if I am able or willing to. But most of all, I can be the face, out of all the many faces that pass, that doesn't look away.

I try to do that, because that's what kin do for each other. They are kind: They offer help, be it assistance, compassion, generosity, tolerance, understanding, or simply acceptance. I admit that I don't always succeed— some days I am too tired or bitter or busy — but when I do, I feel more like *myself*. As if my acknowledging an outcast's membership in the family of man somehow cements mine.

By the way, that book I discovered when I was five, *The Family of Man?* It's still in print, forty-seven years later. Some things never go out of style.

CHAPTER 3

What Kindness Is — and Isn't

The significant problems we face
cannot be solved by the same level
of thinking that created them.

—ALBERT EINSTEIN

I am sitting in my psychiatrist's office. We have been working together for four years, trying to scotch the depression that — despite 400 mg. a day of antidepressants — sends me into tears of despair every morning in the shower, apparently for no reason.

I like Sam a lot. He is smart and funny and we both love living up in the mountains, which most people don't want to call home because of the hairpin roads and dicey electricity. He has kept me going through the sad disintegration of two relationships and the sudden death of my brother Gil, who I adored. I like Sam so much, in fact, I do not even speak up when he starts falling asleep during our sessions.

This happens during a time when I am having three, four, even five dreams a night. I write them faithfully in the journal I have started keeping at Sam's suggestion. When Tuesday afternoons roll around, I march into Sam's office with my journal, exchange some small talk while sipping tea, then read him the dreams I've had since the previous week.

This is quite an undertaking. I don't have short straightforward dreams like the ones in books on dream analysis. I have convoluted and interminable dreams where one scene leads into another and another and another until an entire fantastical saga has unfolded. My dreams are populated by evil doctors, bears, lieutenant colonels, cars of every persuasion, deer, crocodiles wearing heels and red lipstick, and Chinese grandmothers who try to poison me.

One day during my recitation, I notice out of the corner of my eye that Sam has nodded off. I freeze. This is terrible. My first thought is that he must not find out that I have seen him. He would be too embarrassed. He would feel bad. So I keep on reading, never looking directly at him. Eventually his head droops and he jerks awake. I pretend not to notice this, too.

Week after week I continue reading Sam my dreams and he continues to nod off, just briefly, maybe for two or three minutes every session. Once he gives a little snort and a spurt of panic shoots through me. But, thankfully, he sleeps through his own sound effects. When he does awaken, I am careful to maintain the pace and timbre of my voice so he will not know I am aware of his lapse.

When, a year later, Sam and I have our final session, he asks me to give him feedback on our work together. The perfect opportunity to get this off my chest, right? Not for me. I assure him everything has been wonderful. I don't tell him how I feel about his pipe smoke, his catnaps, or the time he asked me to drive him down the block to the garage to pick up his car before his next client arrived.

☙

Why was I so determined that Sam not find out that he had done something I didn't like? Why didn't I say something, like suggest he drink a little coffee instead of weak green tea? Why wasn't I hurt? Here was my wiry little Citroen-driving, pipe-puffing psychiatrist — who listened to me when no one else did, understood me when no one else did, and cared about me when no one else did — suddenly so bored with the night-blooming fruits of my unconscious that he dozes off while I'm talking. Why wasn't I angry? I was paying the guy $90 an hour (and this was more than a decade ago), for heaven's sake. He could at least have stayed awake!

Why? Because I was trying to be nice to him. Unfortunately, my concept of being nice to Sam required that I be unkind to myself, that I dismiss my own feelings as unimportant, even before they could arise. (The irony is that Sam would have loved it if I'd jabbed him in the side and said, "Yo, Sam! Wake up!" He was always trying to get me to be less "nice" and more real.)

The result of treating myself unkindly was that I unconsciously felt worthless and bitter. I was in denial that anything was wrong, but there was. My needs weren't being met. I was repressing my anger and hurt. I was also making myself more and more depressed. All of which seriously undermined my ability to be kind. It is very, very hard to be kind when we are stressed out. And in my experience, whenever I try really hard to be nice, I end up stressed out.

I think we have been sold a bill of goods about the importance of being nice — and in the process we have neglected the far greater virtue: kindness. To me, nice doesn't go very deep. It's the mahogany veneer on the dining table. It's the pleasant response, not the authentic one. It's smiling with one's face but not one's heart.

The dictionary confirms the distinction between "nice" and "kind." Webster tells us that nice means "pleasing and agreeable...courteous and polite," while "kind" means "friendly, generous or warm-hearted, sympathetic and understanding, humane, tolerant."

When we were little, we were told, "Be nice." This meant, "Don't grab Susie's teddy bear," and "Share your crayons — including the purple one, young lady." That's fine. Children need to learn to be considerate of others. But as we get older, the lesson of "Be nice" often gets subtly re-interpreted as "Agree with people" and "Do what others want you to."

Here's an example of nice vs. kind, as I see it. Being nice is going to a gory stalker movie (which I loathe) because a lonely friend really, really wants me to. Being kind is inviting that person over to dinner or taking a hike together instead. When I am kind, my lonely friend gets the companionship they need, and I don't end up scared out of my wits — and having paid for the privilege. Kindness includes kindness to myself, a subject we'll talk a lot more about in Chapter 10.

Is this just a semantic issue of interest only to word fanatics like me? Does the average person make a distinction between being nice and being kind? A friend who volunteers at a hospital asked several nurses and caregivers if they thought there was a difference between being nice and being kind. Nearly 100 percent said no.

End of story? Not by a long shot. A week or so later, these same folks began to drift back to her, saying they'd been thinking some more about her question. As it turned out, they'd been thinking quite a lot.

"To me, niceness is something that's easy to do," said Max, a certified nursing assistant. "It doesn't take much. But kindness really *takes* something."

"Yeah," said Jessie, another CNA. "I was talking about this with my husband, and kindness, well, it's not just *saying* something. It's taking a step out of your own little kingdom."

Later on, a nurse named Lynn came up to my friend. "That's a really interesting question you asked," she said. "We were talking about it at the nurses' meeting. We decided that nice is cheap and kind costs a little more. When I'm nice to somebody, it's not that big a thing. When I'm kind to someone, it feels big to me. I feel good and I know something *happened*."

One of the things that stood out when my friend told me about this was that people got involved with the question. They talked about it with each other over the course of several days. They took it home and discussed it with their partners. They even spent time on it at a staff meeting. The question not only intrigued them, they sensed it was important.

One woman who was asked this question said right away that yes, there was a difference between being nice and being kind. The woman's name is Debra. She is the grown daughter of an elderly man who has been in decline for the past year. The difference, Debra explained bluntly, is this: "'Nice' is fake. 'Kind' brings tears to my eyes."

Debra's response may sound severe, but consider her situation. She is married, works a full-time job, and visits her father four to seven nights a week. He has dementia. To someone under that kind of pressure, "nice" is useless, like throwing a drowning woman a fluffy pink towel instead of a life preserver.

What Debra needs is genuine kindness: someone to help her understand her father's illness and show her how to work the system so he gets better care. Someone to cook meals and stick them in her freezer. Someone to give her a backrub, a pedicure, or a ride in the country to enjoy the wildflowers. Most of all, she needs someone to really listen while she talks about how it feels to see your beloved father in pain, but unable to tell or show you where he hurts.

I'm not anti-nice. What I'm against is being nice when it requires us to suppress our authentic selves. I'm against acting nice when it is motivated by the belief that other people's needs and feelings are more important than ours. Why? Because suppressing our authentic selves and valuing others' needs *instead* of taking care of our own undermines our ability to be kind. It's simple: If we do not feel good about ourselves, we will find it very hard to take the time and effort to be good to someone else.

I think this is because kindness is essentially a creative and inspired act. It is born of empathy, commitment to one's values, and a healthy sense of self. It requires that we make a conscious choice to act, then take that action. It often involves a spiritual connection. How likely is it that we can access these powerful parts of ourselves when we are feeling powerless, unloved, worthless, or depressed?

Not that niceness and kindness cannot co-exist. They can. But too often we do something nice and think we have fulfilled our responsibility to the other members of our global tribe.

Ironically, being nice to someone can actually prevent us from being kind to them. If I call Debra and tell her I know she's carrying a heavy load right now and to let me know if there's anything I can do, I will have been nice to her. I will feel I have done something to help.

I may think I am being kind because my intentions are good and I am sincere, but all Debra has received from me is notification of my willingness. She hasn't actually gotten any relief. But I won't see that. I won't look deeply into Debra's situation and see that people who are overwhelmed rarely have the energy to figure out what they need that could be done for them by someone else. Nor will I check with Debra's husband or best friend to find out what's needed — and then act on it — because, to my way of thinking, I have already done something. If Debra doesn't take me up on my offer, my job is done.

I hope you will tussle a little with the distinction between being nice and being kind. I think it's a hugely important question for all of us. Niceness is not going to save the world. Kindness just might.

∽

If kindness isn't being nice, what is it? That's a little harder to say. We certainly know kindness when we experience it. It opens our hearts. It gives us hope and courage to deal with the hard things in our lives.

Kindness can take the form of a stranger tapping on someone's car window and uttering six words, or a crew of volunteers spending their Saturdays donating sweat equity so a poor family can afford their own home.

You might try a little experiment with yourself, your kids, or a friend. Take a week and see how many acts of kindness you each see, hear about, or personally experience. Make a note of them and report to each other every evening.

When I tried this, kindness seemed pretty thin on the ground at first. But as the days went by and I fine-tuned my kindness receptors, I noticed more and more kindness at work in the world. I found myself stretching my concept of kindness. I went from looking for the obvious to noticing the subtle. I developed a talent for seeing kindness wherever it arose — and in whatever unlikely form it took.

Have you ever learned a new word and then come across it again — and again — almost right away? That's how it is with kindness. Once we have learned how to recognize kind acts, we see them everywhere. Like cruelty (if someone has just hurt us) or Dalmatians (if we have just gotten one), the world seems positively teeming with them.

Here's how it works: The more kindness we see, the more kindness we see. This has to do with the way our minds learn new things. The brain most easily acquires new data if it can attach the new information to information it has already stored. It's like trying to file a piece of paper in a filing cabinet. If there's already a folder for that type of information, we pop the paper in it. If there's no appropriate folder— well, I don't know about you, but I usually toss the darn paper into the recycling bin. I don't store it. That's why new paradigms are so hard to grasp: There's nowhere to put them.

So, if our brain has already got a folder labeled "Acts of Kindness," any new incidents of kindness we come across will be more easily noticed and remembered.

This information-storage process is true for beliefs as well as facts and concepts. As Deepak Chopra puts it, it's not that seeing is believing; it's that believing is seeing. If we don't believe kindness exists, we won't see it if it licks us on the nose. But if we believe that kindness is alive and well, we will see it everywhere. And seeing kindness all around us fuels our own capacity for being kind: Kindness, like misery, loves company.

ಌ

CHAPTER 4

The Enemies of Kindness

You can't let your heart go bad like that,
like sour milk. There's always a chance
you'll want to use it later.

— HALLIE NOLINE
IN BARBARA KINGSOLVER'S *ANIMAL DREAMS*

The man who runs the repair shop shakes his head and shoves the bill for a new ignition over the counter toward the middle-aged woman standing there. Then he turns away to examine the row of work orders hanging on the pegboard wall. After a moment or two, when the woman does not leave the service desk, he says over his shoulder, "There's nothing more I can do, lady."

I wash my hands of you is what he means, Annie thinks. She pulls open the grimy glass door and walks back outside, where the temperature is hovering around twenty degrees. Even with the ignition fixed, she can't drive her car the fifteen miles to her home. It doesn't have license plates. They were missing when the cops finally recovered the car — now emblazoned with black flames and an obscene hood ornament — last week.

The big shot behind the counter claims the hitch on his tow truck is too big to hook up her '88 Honda. He has told her to call AAA, but they won't tow her car because it's still "drivable," even though it doesn't have license plates. But she can't pick up new plates at the DMV: The old plates were from her former home in Texas. And the DMV here in Connecticut won't register the car until they see a Texas driver's license with her picture on it, not just the temporary one that was issued after she lost her wallet in the pre-Christmas rush. Nor can she leave the car at this garage; she's already had to pay the storage fees at the impound lot, plus the cost of replacing the ignition, and her checking account is nearly empty.

Annie is about to retreat to the grimy, pin-up-infested toilet so no one will see her burst into tears of frustration when one of the mechanics' go-fers comes over. He wears a stained blue coverall with the garage logo stitched over the pocket. From his face, Annie guesses he is from Mexico. It's a sensitive face, she notices.

Glancing around to see if his boss is looking, the mechanic's go-fer whispers, "I call Triple A for you. They oughta tow. Too much bad happen for you."

Annie just stares at him. His accent is so heavy, she's not sure she has heard him correctly. Her doubt must show on her face, because the go-fer adds quietly, "I say ignition no work. Is okay. I know someone." Fifteen minutes later, a tow truck carrying a driver and an Hispanic man rolls into the repair yard. "Gimme your card and stay here," the mechanic's go-fer tells Annie. She fishes her AAA membership card out of her purse and hands it over.

The driver, a white guy in creased chinos and a down jacket, climbs out of his tow truck with a clipboard and walks toward the mechanic's go-fer. He takes the AAA card from the silent man.

"This the car?" asks the tow truck driver.

The mechanic's go-fer shrugs.

"Do we have a key?"

The go-fer shrugs again.

"Does the ignition work?" the driver asks impatiently.

Again the shrug.

"Does...the...ignition...work?" repeats the driver, with emphasis on each word.

This time, there's no response at all.

"Dumb bastard," the driver growls. "What about the registration. Where's that?"

The go-fer shakes his head vigorously.

"Hell! I gotta see the registration," the driver says. "Lemme talk to your boss."

Another vigorous head-shake. The expression on the go-fer's face is one of utter incomprehension.

"That does it," the driver declares, slamming his clipboard against his thigh. "I'm outta here."

Now the go-fer bursts into furious speech. "No go! No can leave car here!"

"Look, buddy," says the tow-truck driver, "I cannot tow this car without seeing the — "

"IS MUST GO!" the go-fer snarls, eyes flashing like a Mayan chief who's about to slit the throat of a hated enemy. "More car come. More car, more car. Is must go! MUST GO!"

The driver sighs, then looks back at his tow truck to discover that the Hispanic guy who rode shotgun has just finished hooking up Annie's Honda to the hoist. "Hey!" the driver calls out.

The guy looks up and grins, showing four missing teeth, front and center. "Is done!" he shouts.

The driver stalks back to his tow truck in silence.

Behind him, the mechanic's go-fer gives the Hispanic man a little wave and smiles shyly at Annie. "Go! Go!" he says, with a hurry-up gesture. "He take you."

Annie is dumbfounded. "Thanks, but why did you...." The mechanic's go-fer looks into her eyes, raises a fist, and thumps his heart. Twice.

"Yes," says Annie, touching her own chest. "Me too. But why don't other people?"

The go-fer shakes his head.

"They no gots the time."

❧

I think a lot of us would agree that time is one of the biggest enemies of kindness. We don't have enough time to do what we need to do, let alone the time to be kind to others. We are too busy.

Who else is in the lineup of suspected enemies? Fear is there, along with anger, pain, hatred, selfishness, self-importance, cynicism, stress, exhaustion, apathy, distrust, denial, risk aversion, pessimism, loss of faith, disdain, self-hatred, shame, and — perhaps the most obstinate of all — unconsciousness. Any one of these can block the impulse to be kind or blind us to the fact that someone is in need of kindness. I am sure with very little effort we could find many others to add to the list.

Some people's lives are ruled by negative feelings and traits like these; the rest of us suffer them in varying degrees from time to time. None of us is immune to their downward pull. It's that thing about being contagious again. Dark feelings are contagious, as are dark acts.

For example, is there any doubt hatred is contagious? Look at mob violence, whether in the American South or pre-war Germany. What about fear, denial, apathy, or risk aversion? Consider the murder of Kitty Genovese in Queens in 1964, when thirty-eight people in an apartment house overlooking the scene of the crime watched — for 30 minutes — while a man raped and knifed the young woman to death. Not a single person tried to stop it, cried out for help, or called the police. Fear (*I might get hurt*), denial (*It'll stop soon and she'll be all right*), apathy (*This kind of thing happens all the time*), and risk-aversion (*I'm not getting involved*) held them back, apparently by mutual if unspoken consent.

These are pretty extreme cases. Let's look at what appear to be lesser enemies of kindness. When we are under pressure at home (stress), worn out at the end of the day (exhaustion), mad about something (anger), or simply daydreaming (unconsciousness), do we let other drivers merge onto the highway in front of us? Do we concede the parking space we both came upon at the same time?

Unconsciousness was also Scrooge's downfall, or at least that's how his creator saw it. In *The Christmas Carol*, Charles Dickens has the Ghost of Christmas Present say to the miser, "I'm beginning to think you've gone through life with your eyes closed." The danger in unconsciousness is that we don't *know* our eyes are closed. Sometimes it takes a cataclysm to open them.

How about some other lesser enemies of kindness? When we feel bad about ourselves (how we look, perhaps, or something we've said or done), or feel worthless, unlovable, or loathsome, do we do *anything* for others, even open a door for someone carrying groceries in both arms? Not me. Not when I feel that way. Instead I duck my head and walk on, pretending I can't see the person and they can't see me. I feel too bad about myself to come out of my shell.

Disdain is certainly an enemy of kindness. No town's big enough for the two of them. Several years back, I read a book review in *The New York Times* about an autobiography that focused on the author's spiritual journey. The reviewer described the central part of the book as "screamingly terrible." Not poorly written, egotistical, or shallow (which might actually have told us what the reviewer found objectionable), but "screamingly terrible." What is that if not a clarion call to join the writer of the review in disdaining this man?

Certainly, the *Times* editors (who did not question the use of these words, nor even require the reviewer to provide details of what she objected to) had caught the disdain disease. They too were laughing at the author.

I found it ironic that the reviewer was an author herself. Had she no empathy for the damage a writer can suffer from a cruel review? Obviously not. Being empathetic would not have precluded her from writing a negative review. But it would have prevented her from ridiculing the poor author. Empathy is an ally of kindness. So are a strong sense of self, courage, the willingness to act, and a sense of personal power. We'll talk about them in the chapters to come.

I want to say one more thing about the enemies of kindness before we move on. Most of them are paper tigers. In reality, they are under our control. Anger? We can feel it, express it, and let go of it. Disdain? We can recognize our own human failings and transform our disdain into empathy. Cynicism, pessimism, and hatred? They are all optional.

Shame and self-hatred will yield to counseling; unconsciousness to therapy or meditation; distrust and loss of faith to prayer. I know I am making the defeat of the enemies of kindness sound simple. It's not simple. But it *is* within our power. Whenever something happens to "make" us feel bad or crazy or hurt, we have the power to choose our response. Nothing can "make" us react or feel a certain way, except perhaps in the first few seconds after a provocation when the physiological imperative to throttle, wince, or run away demands to be felt.

There are two more enemies of kindness that deserve special mention: the first because it affects so many of us, the second because its damage goes so deep.

The first is time. Too much to do, too little time to do it. Too many demands. Too little energy. How many people do you know who don't feel strapped for time?

I know *I* feel the time crunch. The funny thing is, the person with the biggest say in how I spend my time is me. I know this is not true for everyone, but bear with me. I notice that I tend to pile up errands and commitments, then try to squeeze them into days that are already packed tight. I start thinking that the stop I wanted to make at the shoe store is a "must." I completely lose sight of the fact that many of the things I "have to" do, I don't really have to do — or I don't have to do them exactly when I planned to.

This is true for socializing, too. When I have the energy to enjoy spending time with people, I do. When I thought I would have the energy on a given day at a given time, but discover that I don't, I call my friends and reschedule. No blame on their part, no guilt on mine. Just me taking responsibility for the fact that when my schedule is crazy, it's usually because I'm crazy to be trying to stick to it. I wonder if this is ever the case for you.

Another approach to defeating this particular enemy of kindness, which we'll call busyness, is with the use of a two-letter word: No. It works quite well, whether directed at our colleagues, families, partners, or — the toughest enemy he faced, according to Mahatma Gandhi — ourselves. Whether spoken kindly or abruptly, "No" is an extremely effective tool for deciding and prioritizing how we will spend our time — and creating more breathing space in our lives. Again, this is about being kind to yourself. If you try it and "No" doesn't work, try "No!" or even better, "NO!" And be sure to say it to yourself before you schedule your life away and there's nothing left of you but your DayTimer.

All this no-saying may not sound very kind. But "No" is not about refusing to be kind because you "need space." It's about refusing to do things that aren't worth your energy, *and* it's about finding a way to be kind to others while also being kind to yourself. Otherwise, we risk killing the goose that lays the golden eggs.

The second enemy that deserves special mention, the one whose damage goes so deep, is loss of faith. I don't mean faith in God specifically, but faith in life. Faith that life is good. That goodness is there, albeit lying doggo (as the British would say) beneath the ebb and flow of everyday events. This is the faith that was restored on that sweltering bus in Chicago when people packed shoulder to shoulder heard the story about a female gorilla who saved a little boy. It's the faith that at heart, people are good, as even Holocaust victim Anne Frank believed.♥

We have seen in the story of Tovah, the young woman on the bus, how having this kind of faith engenders kindness. Does that also mean that losing it destroys our desire to be kind? Let's take a look.

In 1968, a psychology professor at Columbia University conducted a study to determine what percentage of people in a big city were altruistic. Specifically, what percent would do something selfless — give up found money, in this case — for the benefit of a stranger? Harvey A. Hornstein and his crew of assistants

---

♥ The entry in her diary reads, "It's difficult in times like these: Ideals, dreams, and cherished hopes rise within us, only to be crushed by grim reality. It's a wonder I haven't abandoned all my ideals, they seem so absurd and impractical. Yet I cling to them because I still believe, in spite of everything, that people are truly good at heart." Anne wrote these words three weeks before her family was arrested and she was sent to Bergen-Belsen, where she died of typhus some five weeks before the camp was liberated.

spread across New York and "lost" forty wallets a day, each one containing faked personal documents and small sums of money. The study went on for months and the results were surprisingly consistent over time: 45 percent of the wallets were mailed back to the owners week after week.

But, as can happen in research, the authors of the study discovered something they weren't looking for. The altruism rate of 45 percent dropped to zero — *zero* — for wallets "lost" on June 4, 1968. During that night, Senator Robert F. Kennedy — the only viable candidate challenging Republican President Richard Nixon — was shot to death at close range by Sirhan Sirhan. It was only two months after the assassination of Dr. Martin Luther King.

It was the darkest of acts, a murder that affected the freedom of the people to elect the president of their choice. One of its results, an apparently universal loss of faith in goodness, went very deep. It deadened the impulse to kindness among random men and women in the country's largest city.

As we grieved over this assassination, we imagined the family's pain. Robert was the second Kennedy son murdered in office in less than five years. We felt for his mother and father and for his brother, Edward F. Kennedy. Once the youngest of three, he was now the sole surviving son. The nation, Democrats and opposition parties, showed great kindness to the Kennedys, as we had in 1963 when JFK was assassinated.

Our kindness flowed from our ability to share the thoughts and feelings of the grieving family. This ability, without which kindness would not exist, is called empathy.

By the way, the set-back suffered in the return rate of "lost" wallets in New York City was only temporary. Despite whatever the primarily Democratic people of New York City felt about the second assassination of a good man in two months — grief, anger, denial, cynicism, loss of faith — they did not hang onto it. In the days following the Kennedy shooting, the average rate of recovery for "lost" wallets went right back up to 45 percent. Apparently the enemies of kindness were not strong enough, even this time, to block the human capacity for empathy.

CHAPTER 5

It All Starts With Empathy

I can be of no real help to another unless I see
that the two of us are in this together, that all
of our differences are superficial and
meaningless, and that only the countless ways
we are alike have any importance at all.

—HUGH PRATHER IN THE FOREWORD
TO *LOVE IS LETTING GO OF FEAR*

The young man sitting a few tables away in the
deserted hospital cafeteria looks about nineteen. It's
1:30 in the morning, and he's not wearing a hospital
uniform. He's clearly a visitor. Being at a hospital this late

means something serious is going on, and for him it must be more than serious. He is crying.

A woman in her early thirties watches him and frowns unhappily. Her name is Katy James, and she doesn't want to have to help this kid. She's hungry and tired. She doesn't particularly like teenagers. She just wants to be left alone with the Coke and Doritos she got from the cafeteria vending machine — alone, where she can blank out the image of her sister-in-law's head, wrapped in bandages that have left her unable to see, speak, or hear. Vicki has just come through twelve hours of brain surgery. Once she recovers from the operation, she'll be fine — for a while. Until the tumor starts putting pressure on her brain again.

The thought of the future sits in Katy's stomach like a lump of coal. She knows that upstairs, her brother Jim is talking softly to his wife while their Great Dane, Milo, is probably trying to climb into the hospital bed. Vicki's first voluntary movement after surgery was a faint smile when Milo nuzzled her hand. Katy felt good when she and Jim were talking the interns into letting them sneak Milo onto the ward. Like she was part of their little family. But down here, she's all alone again. The story of her life.

Katy looks out the corner of her eye at the young man. He's still crying. The rest of the dimly lit cafeteria is empty. She eats another couple of Doritos. She's not one for talking to strangers. What would she say? Besides, there must be somebody here with him. She takes a swallow of Coke.

But her mind won't let go of this kid. What if there isn't anyone with him? What if he feels as alone as she's feeling? That makes her stomach hurt too. But this is pain Katy can do something about.

She waits a few minutes to get up her courage, then takes the plunge. She pushes back her chair, walks over to the young man's table, and asks if he wants to talk.

He does. His mother is in a coma. She was in a catastrophic car accident three weeks ago and has been unconscious ever since. The family doesn't know what they're going to do.

The young man asks Katy why she's there. She tells him about Vicki and Jim and Milo. Then she mentions how Vicki responded to Milo's touch. The young man's face lights up. He asks Katy if she'll bring Milo to his mom's room. His mom had a Great Dane when she was a kid, he says, and named her Betty Blue because sometimes her fur looked blue.

The next night, Katy gets Milo on a long leash and takes her to the mother's room. Milo seems to know why he's there. He walks up to the woman's bed and nuzzles her hand. When there's no stroking in return, Milo sits back. It's like he's evaluating the situation. Then he stands up, puts his front paws over the bed railing, and nuzzles under the woman's chin. Still no response.

So Milo gets down off the bed and thrusts his nose under the woman's arm, lifting it a good three inches. There's a small but discernible petting in response.

From then on, every night that Katy and her brother visit the hospital, she takes Milo to see the young man's mother. Within a week, the woman has come out of her coma.

ଔ

Did a miracle happen? I think it did. But which miracle are we talking about? I see two extraordinary events in this story. The woman coming out of her coma, that's the obvious one. But what about Katy, who steps out of her sadness and isolation to offer help to a young man who's crying? Without Katy's miracle, the comatose woman would never have had the chance to feel Milo's huge muzzle lifting her apparently lifeless arm.

The seeds of kindness cannot sprout unless they are planted in the rich soil of human empathy. When Katy noticed the young man crying in the cafeteria, she felt empathy for him. She knew what it was like to feel that bad. She had walked a mile in his shoes, and they had hurt her too.

Empathy is the starting point for every act of kindness. Without it, not much happens. With it, miracles of connection are possible. C.S. Lewis expressed this when he wrote, "Friendship is born at the moment when one person says to another, 'What, you too? I thought I was the only one.' " I think we have all had this experience, when a stranger becomes a brother or sister, when we recognize our kinship because we have been through the same hell.

This is why support groups, whether for kicking alcohol, surviving breast cancer, or coping with aging parents, work so well. All the participants discover they are not alone and other people *care* about their struggles because they've been there themselves.

I used to go to a support group every week for people who were molested when they were children. It was tough to get myself there — it would have been so much easier to go home and zone out with a good mystery. But talking about those terrible years to a room full of men and women who had shared similar experiences gave me a kind of relief I didn't get from talking to even my closest friends. There was a deep connection between those of us seated in a circle on folding chairs in the basement of that church. And it wasn't a sick connection. It wasn't about glorying in our pain or hanging onto our wounds. It was about being heard and understood. It was about healing and moving on with our lives.

One night, I walked into the brightly painted meeting room — ironically, it doubled as a day-care center — and was forced to take the last seat, which was next to a man in his late sixties. This man had never been to our group before, and I felt instantly hostile toward him. (Later I would realize I reacted that way because he was the same age as one of the men who molested me. Right then, though, I wanted to yell at him to get out.) Who *is* he, I silently demanded. He doesn't belong here. He's probably a child molester who came here just for kicks.

I pulled my chair away from his until I bumped into the woman on the other side of me. I felt sick and cold. I refused to take a turn to speak. This went on until three minutes before the end of the meeting, when the man finally spoke. His voice was cracked with age and shame. After saying that he had never spoken of these events before, he gave us the barest outline of the pain he had carried for more than sixty years.

When he was done, I looked at him differently. He's not a perpetrator, I thought. He is one of us. And he had been for the entire meeting. Everything else I had made up. I understand now why I reacted this way, but the fact remains that I didn't question my reaction at the time. I just saw this man through the filter of my childhood and locked him out of my heart.

When people started getting up to fold their chairs and stack them against the wall, I turned to him and said, "I'm glad you came tonight." He nodded, folded up his chair, and left the room. I don't think he ever came back.

Empathy is an antidote to my small-minded self. It stretches me. It changes my perspective. It makes me into a bigger person with a bigger heart and a bigger view of the world.

"One of the first signs of empathy is the emerging sense that you and I are *we*," writes psychologist Robert J. Furey in *The Joy of Kindness*. "That somehow, even though appearances may suggest otherwise, we belong to the same tribe. A tribe that has a language in common, the language of human feelings. The more feelings...the greater our vocabulary. Someone with a large vocabulary has the ability and the sensitivity to connect with virtually anyone." ♥

This is why denial is such a significant enemy of kindness. If we refuse to feel our feelings (usually the painful ones), we shut the door on empathy. We cut ourselves off from others, especially people who are suffering and need our help.

This came up for me in the days following the devastating terrorist attacks of September 11, 2001. American flags appeared everywhere: on cars, store windows, personal flagpoles, clothing. I ached for the people who were killed or wounded in the attacks, but I ached too for the innocent people in the Middle East who would surely suffer when we went in search of justice. I felt for the women and children, for the blameless families living in huts, with barely enough to eat, who would soon be killed or wounded when we bombed them "back into the Stone Age," as some put it. It seemed to me that the people demanding we pulverize an entire country in retaliation for an attack by a small team of well-trained terrorists — terrible though it was — were going on the offensive so they wouldn't have to feel

---

♥ This excellent book, published in 1993 by Crossroad Publishing in New York, is out of print, but used copies can be found online.

what the terrorists had just forced us to face: our own vulnerability.

So I wasn't drawn to put an American flag alone in my window. What I wanted to display was a combination of Old Glory and the Earth Flag, the flag that shows the dazzling image of our blue-green earth taken during man's first walk on the moon. I love our country and I am fiercely proud of the freedom that is our birthright, but I believe that first and foremost I'm a citizen of the world. Yes, my country had fallen victim to terrorist acts, but I didn't want my world to fall victim to our nation's need for vengeance.

Several weeks after the attacks, I decided I had to act on my beliefs. I found a web site where I could buy an Earth Flag and placed my order.♥ A week later, a young woman from the company called me to say it would be a while 'til I received my flag. Since 9/11, they had been overwhelmed with orders.

Is empathy for others something we learn or something we are born with? Until 1990, it was widely believed children do not begin to act altruistically until age seven. Freud said children are not altruistic until they are old enough to act based on societal values instead of their impulses. Child expert Jean Piaget held that children could not be altruistic until they developed the cognitive skills that would enable them to see things from someone else's point of view.

♥ It's www.earthflag.net.

But world-renowned psychologist and scholar Piero Ferrucci disagrees. In his book *Inevitable Grace,* he cites a study done with children ages eighteen months to two years. In some 1,500 incidents where the toddlers were exposed to someone else's mild suffering, like a parent coming home tired or disappointed, or someone getting a minor burn from a hot stove, the majority of these very young children wanted to help or comfort the person who was hurting.

"Empathy and a spontaneous feeling of concern for others are not imposed from outside, nor are they factors of mental maturity, Ferrucci writes. "Instead they are natural, original attitudes of our being."

"I've been watching young children most of my life and they are more often kind to each other than unkind. The early instinct to help someone is powerful," writes Vivian Gussin Paley, a retired kindergarten teacher whose numerous widely respected books on young children are published by Harvard University Press.

If Ferrucci and Paley are right — and I certainly want to believe they are; don't you? — then what happens to our instinctive empathy for others when we grow up? Does the dearth of kindness in our adult world mean that although we may feel empathy, we often choose not to act on it? And if so, why?

What gets in our way?

C₈

CHAPTER 6

Who Am I, Anyway?

You don't get to choose how you're going to die.
Or when. You can only decide how
you're going to live. Now.

—JOAN BAEZ

It is April in San Francisco. I am walking with three
friends early one evening toward the lecture hall where
novelist Barbara Kingsolver is going to speak. As we make
our way down Van Ness Avenue, we come upon a
homeless man sitting on the sidewalk, his legs stretched
out in front of him. A small spotted dog sits at attention
by his side.

Automatically, I smile and walk over to the little dog. "Oh, aren't you adorable," I murmur as I stroke his head. He looks up at me with chocolate brown eyes and wags his feathery tail. "What a nice dog," I exclaim to his owner. Then I notice my friends waiting and turn away to rejoin them.

Ten yards farther along Van Ness, we come to a red light. As my friends and I stand and wait, I frown, thinking about the man and his dog. That dog was so dear, I hope he gets enough to eat. I wonder where they sleep.

Then a different voice in my head says, *Did you notice that you smiled at the dog and not at the man?*

Oh, but the dog was so cute! And there are so many homeless people on the streets of San Francisco. Heck, he's probably a pro — he's even using his dog as a marketing ploy. I hate marketing ploys.

I check the light. It is still stubbornly red.

You smiled at the dog and not at the man.

After a long silence, I admit it.

I did. That's not right.

You usually give homeless people some money. Why not him?

He'd probably use it for booze.

Do you know that for sure?

Well, look at him.

If he does spend it on booze, is that something you can control?

No.

Is it even any of your business what people do with the gifts you give them?

I guess not....

He might buy hot soup or dog food. You don't really know what he'll do, do you?

No.

Will you ever know for sure what he spends your dollar on?

No.

So you can simply decide that he will spend it on hot soup?

I could....

And you'd feel good about having given him the money.

Yes, I would.

So it's up to you whether you feel like you got taken or not.

The voice is right. I am not behaving like the kind and generous person I think I am — and really want to be. I unzip my purse and take out my wallet. One of my friends looks over, slightly alarmed. She lived in New York City for years and knows that you never, never open your purse at night on a dark city street.

I walk back to the man and his dog, bend down, and offer him two dollars. He reaches out and takes it from my hand. Our skin touches. I look in his face.

"Take care and good luck to you."

"Thank you," he says as he looks back.

We have made contact, human to human. Something real has happened, and I feel better. More like myself.

I return to my friends. The light is green now, and as we cross I realize that I have given this man something much more important than money. I have given him a reminder that we are both held in the same web of care and connection, a web that vibrates with love when we choose to be kind.

And he has given that gift to me.

☙

One thing we often overlook about kindness is that it is entirely optional. No one can make us be kind. They can pressure us to do something that looks kind, like donate money to a charity at the office. But every genuinely kind act done in this world is a result of someone having chosen to do it of their own free will.

"The door to the heart," says Robert Furey, "can only be opened from the inside."

Any of the people in the stories I've shared could have ignored the problem they saw. No one hearing about the incident would have asked, "Why didn't you help that person?"

No one except the voice inside them.

The choice to be kind is a private matter concerning our heads, our hearts, and our souls. The voice that got my attention that night in San Francisco was very different from my small-minded self, who thought she was going to get fooled, taken, ripped off. It didn't accuse or argue with me. It simply presented me with the facts of what I had done. It created an opening and invited me in. My small, suspicious self — which I seem to switch into every time I go into a big city — had the choice to listen or not.

Having decided to listen to the voice of my soul, I found myself faced with another choice. Was my small, suspicious self the one I wanted to make the decisions in my life? Did I want to live as if I were a victim waiting to happen? Or did I want to reach for something higher?

Choice is incredibly powerful. On that dark street in San Francisco, I was not only able to choose what to do, I was able to choose how I felt about it. I had the power to decide that my gift would be used well. I could choose to walk away from that man (and his adorable little dog) "knowing" I had made a difference in his evening. Was I fooling myself? If I was, does it matter? Not if I have chosen what I will take away from the experience: a sense of accomplishment at having taken right action. "Right action" doesn't mean correct action. It means action that's right for the values we try to live by. It's "right," as in meeting someone who's right for you.

We come upon crossroads like this all the time. Here we are, cruising along the highway of life, and suddenly we come upon an opening. We see someone in a jam because her car was stolen. We see someone sitting in a darkened cafeteria crying. Do we choose to slow down and help or do we keep going?

The answer to that question is important — to the person who needs help, sure, but it's important to us, too. Maybe even more important. There's a Buddhist verse called the Five Remembrances that explains why this is so. It includes these words: "My deeds are the ground on which I stand."

As we choose which deeds we will do, so we choose our identity, the ground on which we stand. We come to know ourselves in the same way others come to know us: by our deeds. This is why choosing to do kind deeds helps us develop a strong and healthy sense of self.

In order to decide whether we are going to stop and help, we are forced to examine our values. What matters to us? What are the standards we live by? Do we smile kindly at a homeless dog but not at a homeless man? These openings we come upon as we cruise along in our everyday lives, these opportunities for kindness, are the very moments when we get to choose — and change — who we are.

The result of my meeting with the homeless man and his cute dog was that I came to know myself better. I saw through my own "press release" — the belief I hold that I am a kind and generous person. I glimpsed the part of me whose heart went out to a dog but not a man. I had a chance to catch myself in the act. I didn't much like what I learned, but concurrent with the learning came the opportunity to do things differently, to act in alignment with my soul.

This is why kindness is such a powerful path to self-knowledge. The world is our laboratory. It offers us innumerable opportunities to test our mettle. We get to discover how much of us is lead and how is much gold.

And we get the alchemical chance to turn some of our lead into gold.

Kindness not only helps us know our own worth, it increases our sense of worth. When we choose to intervene in someone's life by doing good, we make a difference in someone's life, no matter how small. We are agents of positive change. We *matter*. ♥

The other day I was talking with a group of women I meet with every month, telling them about my theories on kindness and how being kind can make such a difference in our lives.

Alma, who just turned eighty, said with a slight note of surprise, "I was in the store the other day, and when I left, I held the door open for the man behind me."

"How did you feel?" I asked her.

"Good! It felt really good."

"Did you feel more like yourself?"

"Yes," she said with some surprise. "I did."

When we are kind, our words and actions make a statement about our identity. I think this is why we feel more like ourselves. Not only are we acting in alignment with our souls, we are, in effect, saying to the person we are helping, "I am someone who wants you to get out of

---

♥ Be careful about this. While an increased sense of self-worth is the result of being kind, it is a disastrous *reason* for being kind. Doing the right thing for a selfish reason is likely to backfire: We may find our offer of help thrown back in our faces. We can only control the intentions of our kindness, never the results.

this jam." Or, "I am someone who wants you to have money to buy dinner" or "who doesn't want you to give up hope." At heart, an act of kindness is an act of self-expression.

I think Alma felt more like herself for two reasons. First, because she was doing something that expressed who she was. Second, because she was doing something that raised her self-respect. She was out there cruising along and decided to stop and help. She chose to be someone who could hold a door open for someone else, even if she *was* eighty.

One of the amazing things about kindness is how little it takes to make us feel great, whether we are on the receiving end or the giving end. Opening a door for a stranger at the market — not a big deal, right? But it was. Imagine approaching the non-automated door of a grocery store, carrying brown bags in both arms, and there's a very little old lady holding the door open for you. Pretty cool.

When we use kindness as a practice to discover our essential self and learn to live from it, we have two powerful allies at our back. One is our heart, which is the home of love, and the other is our soul, which is the home of Spirit (or whatever you prefer to call it).

I can imagine my heart and my soul sitting in the stands watching me at bat. I am served up an opportunity to be kind — it's a swing and a miss! I walk past the guy sitting on the street. My heart and my soul slap their hands to their foreheads and groan. Another ball speeds toward the plate. This time I connect! I head for first while my heart and my soul knock their beer cans together and drink a sloppy toast.

Our hearts and our souls will always root for us to be kind, to come through in a pinch. No matter how many times we hit foul balls or strike out, they won't boo us. They won't leave the stands in a huff.

They may get frustrated with our game, but they know that as long as we stick with it, we'll grow into players they can be proud of.

In fact, they are betting on it.

A SHORT COURSE IN KINDNESS

ℭ

Chapter 7

Where Courage Comes In

It takes courage for a man to listen to his own
inner goodness and act on it.
Do we dare to be ourselves?
This is the question that counts.

—PABLO CASALS, QUOTED IN O: *THE OPRAH MAGAZINE*

A N operating theater is one of the last places you'd
expect to hear Shakespeare. And it was the very last
place Lisa Derr wanted to end up when she went in for a
routine checkup five months into her first pregnancy.

But it is where she is being wheeled, naked under
the sheet covering her gurney and a little high on pre-
surgery drugs. Lisa clutches at her sheet. She is frantic

with fear — she has never had surgery before — and her heart is aching with more pain than she knew she was capable of feeling.

Just a few hours earlier, her doctor told her that her baby was dead and she needed to have a D&C as soon as possible. Devastated, she called her husband, David, who is now pacing the waiting room.

Men and women in masks and gowns peer down at Lisa's covered form as her gurney is wheeled and locked into position. They know what her situation is and they know what they are going to do. Lisa, however, is almost over the edge. If she hadn't been given the tranquilizer, she'd be screaming. Her baby is dead and strangers with shiny metal instruments are about to probe the most sensitive and private part of her body.

She's feeling disoriented and a little high. Her eyes scan the room and settle on the circular metal light fixtures above her.

"Wow," she mumbles. "They look like two metal breasts."

The anesthesiologist laughs. "Oh, you're a poet!"

"I am," replies Lisa in all seriousness.

"I'm going to put something over your mouth now," he says. Lisa's eyes widen in fear then suddenly she relaxes. Something wonderful is happening.

A couple of hours later, she opens her eyes. David is there, holding her hand.

"Hi there," he says.

"Oh, David..." Lisa begins. Her voice is faint, but she sounds like she's okay. "It wasn't so bad. And I had this dream. I was floating on words. The syllables were coming into me."

David smiles at his wife, the poet.

"Really," Lisa says. "They were like the beautiful sound of music as I faded into black." She pauses, then smiles, "David, I dreamed the anesthesiologist was reciting poetry to me! Shakespeare sonnets."

"He was," her husband says.

∞

You have to be pretty tough to make it through medical school, but you don't have to give up your ability to be kind. Toughness and kindness are not mutually exclusive. Kind people can make tough decisions. Sometimes kindness requires tough decisions. Kindness is not for wimps.

It takes courage to be kind. Kindness makes us vulnerable. When we do something kind, we are opening our hearts (through empathy) and letting ourselves be seen (since kindness is an act of self-expression). That can be pretty risky. There are always people who will laugh or sneer or otherwise try to make us feel bad when we show our vulnerability. My policy is to let as few of those people near me as possible. But sometimes policy can't protect us.

Take this book. It was born through the same sequence of feelings and choices that result in an act of kindness. The process began when I saw — and felt — how desperately we need more kindness in our world. Then I decided to write a book about it. This decision both reflected and strengthened my sense of self.

And frankly, it took courage. If my book were to do any good in the world, I knew I had to speak from my heart, to expose some very personal things about my life and my beliefs, including my spiritual beliefs. I knew some people would laugh at the things I said. Someone *always* laughs. You can count on it.♥

But I had to decide to do it anyway. I had to resolve to navigate by my own compass, not the compass of popularity or approval. I used to live that way and it was no way to live. I was never truly happy. Even when I won acclaim and approval, it was temporary. The next moment I could do something "they" didn't like. What a tightrope to walk. Two directions led to safety, all the others to disaster.

How do we make it past our fears so we can act kindly? We start by acknowledging that those fears exist. We all have them, and we can't disarm them unless we admit they're there. As Mark Twain reminds us, "Courage isn't the absence of fear, it's just not letting fear stop us."

♥ If I am both very lucky and very unlucky, *The New York Times* will decide to review this book — and will assign it to the reviewer who uses descriptions like "screamingly terrible." I'll keep you posted.

Second, remember that everyone who has ever achieved anything in this world has been criticized, mocked, even rejected along the way. Galileo was forced to recant his discovery that the earth moves around the sun. Charles Darwin's agent told him to forget writing about his trip to the Galapagos, no one would want to read it.♥ Even Shakespeare got bad reviews.

Finally, you will discover that even the most sensitive of us can learn to ignore naysayers when we know in our hearts we're doing the right thing.

The courage to steer by our own compass is the first type of courage we need in order to be kind. The second is the courage to silence the fearful part inside that wants to keep us small and safe, and make sure we never, never take risks where we might get hurt. Writer Natalie Goldberg talks about how powerful this part is — and how overcoming it frees us from more than just ourselves. "If you are not afraid of the voices inside you," she writes, "you will not fear the critics outside you."

We all have voices inside that say, "You're asking for trouble," or, "You're going to fail," or, most common of all, "You'll be sorry." These voices have a million ways to warn, criticize, bully, and shame us into not taking risks. It's our job to thank them for their opinions and go do precisely what we want. Because if we don't take risks, we

---

♥ He suggested Darwin do a book on pigeons instead; they were enjoying a sudden surge of popularity among London's city-dwellers.

never grow. We never live. We never discover what we are really capable of.

By the way, these voices are right: We might be sorry. We might fail. Taking risks *does* make us vulnerable. But I think being vulnerable is part of the reason kindness works.

Here's why. By definition, kindness involves two people: one person who needs kindness and one who is willing to give it. So far in this book, we have only talked about the challenges of being the kindness-giver. What about the person on the receiving end?

For most of us, receiving doesn't come easy. Have you ever been involved in a conversation that went like this:

"Let me treat you to dinner tonight."

"Oh, no. You don't have to do that."

"It would be a pleasure."

"Still. That's okay. I can pay for myself."

We seem to feel we aren't worth another person's kindness. And if we get talked into accepting someone's gift, we think we have to pay them back. Lisa, the poet in the story that opens this chapter, was offered free coaching for a year by a prominent marketing consultant who loved her writing and wanted to help her succeed. The first few months they worked together, Lisa kept sending her mentor presents: a book, a CD, some cookies she had made, Belgian chocolates. Finally he called her up and said, "Lisa, stop sending me things. I am doing this because I want to. You don't owe me. Besides, the chocolates melted all over the rest of my mail."

Sound familiar? It does to me. Receiving can feel uncomfortable in the best of circumstances. But what if we are being offered money or clothing or food because we are poor or not warmly dressed or hungry? Because someone looked at us and saw how vulnerable we are? How hard it must be to receive help from someone who looks invulnerable, someone who is well-off, warm, and well-fed.

And how much easier it is to accept someone's kindness when they are meeting us as an equal, when we both have something — perhaps pride, perhaps self-esteem — at risk. Think back to the story about the black woman who saw a young white woman crying in the parking garage. How would the young woman have felt if the black woman had stuck a note under her windshield wiper and walked away instead of tapping on the window and speaking to her face to face?

I can't imagine she would have been as comforted. In speaking directly to the young woman, the black woman allowed herself to be vulnerable. She risked being rejected with an angry gesture or a racial slur. I think her courage in taking this risk was part of what made her act kind. She showed that she cared enough about the young woman's feelings that she was willing to take a risk to help her.

When we risk being kind, we ante up our own humanity. We connect with the people who need our help as kinsmen and women. We offer them genuine human contact and remind them that they are part of the family of man.

Yes, it takes courage to be kind. It calls for exposing ourselves, for putting ourselves on the front lines. That's why it's so important not to be daunted by others' opinions. We must let go of what other people think in order to lead them by example.

Kindness is a revolution that needs as many leaders as possible. When will we know we have succeeded? When we look behind us and see no followers, only people walking beside us, doing their best to meet life with an open heart.

CO

CHAPTER 8

We Act, Therefore We Are

You can't cross the sea merely
by standing and staring at the water.

— RABINDRANATH TAGORE

You wouldn't take her for a warrior. She is 20, a
secretary in a law office. She has just gotten off a long
day's work. Her clothes are modest and well cared for,
her well-polished shoes worn down completely at the
heel. Her name is Marti and she is waiting at the bus stop
early on this January evening because a friend totaled her
car yesterday. It wasn't much of a car, but still....

Marti is also pregnant. When she told her boyfriend
awhile back, he abruptly left her. Marti's manner is quiet

but unashamed. She is looking forward to the baby. In her purse she has booklets and samples of the cosmetics she plans to sell out of her home in addition to her job. Babies are expensive, she knows.

It's already dark out, but looking to her right, she notices a woman stoop and pick up something from the gutter. It's a wallet. The woman starts rifling through it. Marti strides over to her.

"I see you found a wallet," she says, taking it out of the woman's hands. The woman makes a muttered reply, shoves her hands into her pockets, and walks over to the bus stop.

Before Marti can examine the wallet, two dark-skinned young men skid their Jeep Durango to a stop next to her.

"Hey, that's ours!" the driver shouts. "It belongs to my sister."

Marti looks them over, then opens the wallet. The picture on the driver's license shows a fair-skinned woman in her forties with short red hair. She holds the wallet up for the men to see, displaying the driver's license. "*This* is your sister?" she asks indignantly. "She doesn't look like your sister!"

The man in the passenger seat starts to get out of the Jeep. Marti steps quickly back to the bus stop where other people are waiting. The Jeep speeds angrily away, laying rubber.

At home, Marti calls Information to get the phone number of the woman on the driver's license. The number is no longer in service. There is no other form of I.D. in the wallet. So she takes everything out and lays it on the kitchen table. She finds no money, no credit cards. She remembers the woman at the bus stop shoving her hands back into her pockets. There are several business cards and a picture of two dark-haired teenagers smiling. On the back is written, "Love, Danny and Becky."

She examines the business cards and finds one for a man with the same last name as the wallet's owner. He lives on the other side of the country. That means a long-distance call. Marti picks up the phone and dials. It takes two calls to reach a number where someone will take a message.

The next day at work, Marti gets a call from the tourist who lost the wallet. She had been desperate to find it. She needs to fly home the next day, and without any I.D. she can't get on the plane.

The two women meet that afternoon in a parking lot across the street from Marti's office. She can only take a short break from work. The woman takes her lost wallet from Marti's outstretched hand and asks, "Where did you find it?"

Marti tells her the story, including the part about the two men.

"Weren't you afraid?" the woman asks. "What made you do that?"

"It wasn't theirs!" Marti says angrily. "If it ever happened to me, I would want someone to do the same thing."

The woman reaches into her coat pocket and takes out two twenty-dollar bills.

"Would you please accept this? I wish I could give you more, but it's all I have left."

"You don't understand," Marti says. "That's not why I did it." She turns and starts back toward her office.

The woman calls after her. "Will you at least take it for your baby?"

Marti turns and considers. "Yes," she finally says, smiling. "For my baby."

As Marti tucks the two bills in her pocket, the woman asks, "Why didn't you just walk away? It would have been so easy."

"It wouldn't have been the right thing to do," Marti says simply.

☙

I used to think I was a really kind person because I thought kind thoughts. I hadn't realized that thoughts weren't enough. I hadn't realized that kindness required me to actually *do* something.

Two things woke me up, a song and a piece of scripture from the Buddhist canon. The song is John Hiatt's "Through Your Hands," and I first heard its powerful message it on album by Joan Baez.

It tells the story of a daydreamer sitting on a park bench who is startled awake by the ringing of carillon bells. The swelling celestial sound of the bells fills the dreamer's heart and seems to hurl it into the sky, where our poor daydreamer (who has only been imagining a real life, not living one) is gathered into the arms of an angel.

Like a confused and plaintive child turning to its mother, the dreamer asks, "What am I not doing?" The angel responds by sharing one of the great secrets of life. "Your voice cannot command," Baez sings, her own voice as smooth and rich as honey. We listen, thinking, If any voice can command, it must be this one.

But the angel says not. "In time you will move mountains," she tells the dreamer, "and it will come through your hands." The word "come" is drawn out in a mesmerizing succession of notes that lifts the listener's spirit to the skies, much as the dreamer's heart was carried aloft by the ringing of the carillon.

Have you ever had the experience of hearing words — a song or a poem perhaps — that sent chills through your body and brought tears to your eyes? That's when we know we have been struck by truth. This is what happened when I first heard this song. I had bought the album because I wanted to hear the title cut, "Play Me Backwards." But that wasn't what the universe had in mind. Once again, I had stumbled by mistake onto the right path, the path that would take me to something I was supposed to learn.

I didn't understand the lyrics that so moved me. Of course my voice could command! After all, I was a professional writer, a public speaker. I knew I could inspire people, could move them with my words. Of course you can move mountains with your voice! Isn't that what Joan herself does? I thought I had a pretty good argument there. Surely I could forget about that teary little *frisson* I'd experienced.

But I couldn't. It kept happening whenever I heard the song, which was often because I was strangely drawn to play it. I still didn't understand what I was supposed to be doing differently with my life. At the time I was publishing a supportive self-help newsletter for women who were recovering from childhood sexual abuse. Wasn't that enough? Wasn't that "with my hands"? Apparently not, or I wouldn't have had that strong physiological reaction to the words of the song. The body never lies. It doesn't know how.

Now we pass to the second wakeup call I got on the subject of doing, not just talking. It was at least five years later. I was attending a meditation and talk at the home of my Zen teacher, Yvonne Rand. The topic was a Buddhist meditation called the Five Remembrances, the one I mentioned in Chapter 6.

When I go to hear Yvonne speak, I know I will hear something worth chewing on, so I try to listen closely. I was also curious about the subject; I had not heard of the Five Remembrances. But as the discussion proceeded, I was a little disappointed. These remembrances (meaning "things to be remembered") seemed to cover familiar territory in Buddhist thought. They stated that there is no escape from growing old, from getting ill, from dying, or from being separated from our loved ones. I had thought about those concepts before and knew that despite appearances, they were not designed to depress us. To the contrary, they outline the Buddhist path to happiness. These verses aren't saying, "Shoot yourself now, it only gets worse." They are saying, "This is the nature of life, which we cannot avoid or change. Live with these truths in mind and you will experience freedom and happiness. You will not waste your time here on earth. You will cherish the present moment."

That was all well and good, but I had heard it before. I started to listen a little less avidly than usual. Then Yvonne came to the fifth truth that the Buddha asked his students to remember. The full text of it goes like this: "My deeds are my closest companions. I am the beneficiary of my deeds. My deeds are the ground on which I stand."

I jerked back to attention. Deeds? *Deeds?* What about our intentions? Our beliefs? Our thoughts and our words? Buddhist philosophy stresses the importance of these things. What was going on here?

That's when I got it. Those other things *are* important. But they are not the bottom line, if you'll forgive my using a financial metaphor in a spiritual context. What matters is what we *do*. What *action* we take. It's wonderful to think holy thoughts, and I do believe they make a difference in our individual and communal lives. But it's not enough.

Our deeds are our closest companions. They accompany us wherever we go. For good or for ill, we can never be free of them. We are the beneficiaries of our deeds. We inherit their effects. We suffer — or enjoy — the consequences of our deeds.

This wisdom on the importance of our actions is not something we can dismiss as being foreign, unchristian, or out of date. Contemporary thinkers have tried to teach us the same thing.

Psychologist Piero Ferrucci says, "No action leaves us the same as before. Whether it be stealing or making a gift, heroism or eroticism, restraint or spontaneity, everything we do leaves its mark on us...Just as streams engrave their course into the earth, so our actions mold our character. We are what we have done."

The "longshoreman philosopher," Eric Hoffer, tells us: "Help your sister's boat across the water, and yours too will reach the other side. Kindness is its own motive. We are made kind by being kind."♥

Finally, I'll share with you what my first writing teacher, Grace Paley, told twelve eager college freshmen in 1968, when she unknowingly offered a motive that might lead even the most selfish of people into being kind. When all is said and done, Grace said, "You get the face you deserve."

♥ From his book *The Passionate State of Mind.*

ɔ຅

CHAPTER 9

The Connection Between

Kindness and Power

Understanding kindness means accepting our
personal power. If you see your place in the
universe, *really see it*, you will not be struck by your
insignificance. Rather, you will be awed by
your...power to build and contribute.

—ROBERT J. FUREY, *THE JOY OF KINDNESS*

Gabrielle parks the Volvo on a side street in Berkeley,
unloads the things she will need for class, and locks
the door. She must walk three blocks to reach the
meeting room where her students have gathered tonight.

The air is chilly and the streets are damp from a day of welcome winter rain.

She is thinking about her garden, mostly dormant now, and whether she should move the upright rosemary to a sunnier spot, when her legs suddenly go out from under her and she lands on her back, her belongings flying.

Her heart is momentarily racing. It's no small thing to take a fall at night on an empty city street, especially when you are sixty. She feels defenseless lying there on the wet pavement.

From down the street, she hears the sound of running feet. Two men are coming toward her in the dark. Suddenly they are grabbing her by the arms.

"Are you okay?" asks one man.

"We saw you go down," says the other. "That was quite a fall."

As she is lifted to her feet, Gabrielle can just make out the men's faces. Their cheeks are unshaven and creased, their hair tangled, their clothes a mismatched jumble of ragged plaids and moth-eaten woolens. Her saviors are two Berkeley street people.

ଓ

Kindness has the capacity to turn the powerless into the empowered. No matter how the two men who helped Gabrielle had felt about themselves the moment before they ran to her, we can be sure they stood taller afterward. They had come through for someone. They had helped someone in need. They had been kind. My guess is that they felt powerful. Not "powerful" as in wielding power. But "powerful" as in influential, capable, effective, energetic, able, and competent.

When I told my best friend I was writing a chapter about kindness as the ultimate path to power, there was a significant silence on her end of the line.

"No, not power as in forced marches or hostile takeovers," I hastened to add. "Not power *over*. Power *within*."

Power has been so misused over the centuries, the word now has a negative connotation. Dictators are powerful. Corporations are powerful. The CIA is powerful. Big insurance companies are powerful. Nowadays, "power" pushes people around and they have no choice but to take it.

But power is simply a type of energy. It can be used for good or ill, just as a powerful car can be used to run someone down or race to the airport to deliver a transplant organ.

We have all seen the effect of the power of love in our own lives and in the lives of those around us. Prayer also has power — as do beauty, truth, and goodness. The stories in this book are filled with powerful people, like the gentle-hearted anesthesiologist, the mechanic's go-fer, the pregnant defender of lost wallets, the ragged men in Berkeley.

Doing the right thing in the face of the odds makes us feel our power. Whether our acts of kindness are quiet ones, like Katy offering her help to the young man in the hospital cafeteria, or fierce and passionate ones, like Marti fending off thieves, their legacy is a strong sense of personal power. This is the reward that comes when we live by our own best lights, as Quaker author Parker Palmer puts it.

Committing acts of kindness shows us the power that we have — over ourselves and our choices, and over whether this world is a cruel or wondrous place to live. All of the people who benefited from the kind acts I've told you about got more than the practical help they were given.

Remember Holly's story of being slipped a sandwich in the deli when she was exhausted from caring for her mom? She said she felt like she'd been given a shot of adrenaline: "It *carried* me...I swear the molecules rearranged inside me." Later, looking back on that act of kindness, she said, "It passes in a breath, but you feel it forever." After Gabrielle told her students the story of the street people rescuing her, she said, "When I saw their faces, they fell into my heart."

The increased sense of power that comes from kindness doesn't necessarily depend on whether our kind acts have the effect we hope for. In fact, there will be times when we cannot know exactly what effect our actions have had. We will feel empowered all the same. I wouldn't have thought this was true until I talked to people who'd experienced it.

When I asked my circle of friends for stories of kindness for this book, Ruiko told me about the time she was a sophomore at Penn State and worked in the library. She noticed that one of the other students who worked there was looking ill. He was pale and drawn, his body thinner. She asked him if he was sick. He said that he and his wife hated living in the area and he had stopped eating so they could save money to leave. Ruiko went home and thought this over. In the morning she brought the young man three sandwiches: egg salad, tuna fish, and peanut butter and jelly. "The next day," she told me, "his friend came up and said, 'John doesn't like mayonnaise. He threw the egg salad and tuna fish in the trash and ate the peanut butter.' "

Hearing this, I thought, well, that's not a story I would use in the book. But when I looked at Ruiko, she was smiling. She felt good about what she had done for John. Nothing had changed that.

Kindness calls for us to expand many of our capacities. In order to undo my thoughtlessness in smiling at the homeless man's dog but not at the man himself, for example, I had to see through my own "press release" — and confess to what I saw. I had to recognize that I wasn't always the generous person I liked to think I was. I had to expand my capacity for self-examination and my tolerance for my own mistakes. By doing so, I discovered a wealth of power in me: the power to change my thoughts, the power to change my behavior, the power to reach out to someone I'd wronged, the power to treat my small-minded self with compassion.

I think kindness — and personal power — is all about choice. We choose whether to feel empathy for others or to allow anger, denial, or depression to block our capacity for caring. We choose whether to stop and be kind when the opportunity arises. We choose to do what's right despite what others may think or what our own small fears may be. We choose to implement our decision to be kind by taking action.

Never underestimate the power that comes with simply *having* a choice, nor the personal power we feel once we've decided what our choice will be. Viktor Frankl discovered this truth in Auschwitz. The camp inmates were beaten, starved, deprived of sleep, worked beyond endurance, humiliated, hated, and massacred. Yet, as Frankl tells us in *Man's Search for Meaning*, not even the desperately cruel conditions of a concentration camp could take away "the last of the human freedoms — to choose one's attitude in any given set of circumstances, to choose one's own way...." His conclusion is that "Fundamentally...any man can...decide what shall become of him — mentally and spiritually."

There is no greater power than this, and this is the power that choosing kindness gives us.

ca

CHAPTER 10

Don't Forget to Be Kind to Yourself

Self-care is never a selfish act. It is simple good
stewardship of the only gift I have,
the gift I was put on earth to offer others.

—PARKER PALMER, *LET YOUR LIFE SPEAK*

I am lying in bed under my rumpled comforter, one arm curved around my curled-up cat. It is early and I can hear the Oregon juncos chittering in the tall trees outside my bedroom window. I am about to recite the short mindfulness verse I say every morning.

I am very fond of this meditative moment. First, it's a spiritual practice I can do without getting out of bed. Second, the verse is cheerful, a nice balance for those Five

Remembrances verses about growing ill, growing old, losing our loved ones, and dying.

The morning verse goes like this.

Waking up this morning, I smile.
Twenty-four brand new hours are before me.
I vow to live fully in this moment
and to look at all beings with eyes of compassion.♥

This early-morning moment with nature and gentle self-awareness is very pleasant. Partly that's because I think I'm good at keeping the three vows in the verse: the vow to be grateful for the day, the vow to appreciate the present moment, and the vow to be compassionate toward others.

As I begin the verse today, I'm looking out my window. I smile at the soft pink rays of dawn that dapple the peeling trunks of the eucalyptus trees. I feel grateful for the day ahead. I cherish this moment — no problem when moments are as lovely as this.

Then comes a rude awakening. As I start to speak the last line of the verse, in which I vow to look at all beings with eyes of compassion, the words stick in my throat. My gaze has drifted back into the bedroom, and I find myself staring straight into the eyes of a tired, aging, overweight woman whose short gray hair is sticking out at unattractive angles all over her head.

♥ From Thich Nhat Hanh's lovely book of verses, *Present Moment, Wonderful Moment.*

I wince at my reflection in the mirror. I don't like what I see. I think, Do I have to look at *her* with eyes of compassion, too?

The answer, of course, is yes.

· ∞

Why is it that we can be immensely kind to others yet so hard on ourselves? Why don't we realize that when we choose kindness as a way to walk in the world, the path includes kindness to ourselves? Being kind to humanity *includes* being kind to ourselves.

Somehow being kind to ourselves has gotten a bad rap. It gets equated with self-indulgence, selfishness, and self-pity. This is just not true. Being kind to ourselves means taking care of ourselves as we would take care of anyone we loved. Without self-care, we won't have the energy to be kind. Self-care is the cradle of kindness.

I have a fountain in my house, the kind that sits on a tabletop. When the water burbles out the top, it flows down over some fake rocks and splashes gently into a bowl, where the pump sucks the water up again. If the pump gets turned up too high by mistake, water spurts onto the table. Pretty soon, all the water in the fountain has splashed out onto the table. None of it has collected in the bottom of the bowl to rest in a pool until it is sucked back up by the pump. Now the water has started dripping onto the floor. The cats, knowing a good thing when they see one, trot over to bat at the drops of water in midair. The pump seizes up with a metallic snarl. Its motor has burned out. For good. It cannot be repaired.

The same thing happens to us. If we do not take time to rest and replenish ourselves after showering kindness on others, we burn out. Sometimes we burn out for good and never devote energy to others again. That's why self-care is crucial if we want to be kind to others.

When I look back at that morning when I was startled by the haggard "stranger" in my mirror, I not only notice my lack of compassion for her, I notice that she was exhausted. She was running a company dedicated to helping people heal their emotional wounds from childhood. She paid her employees and suppliers (though not herself) on time, treated her customers honorably and kindly, provided free services to her community — and pretty much ignored her own needs. She was working too hard, eating badly, not sleeping enough, and worried about money most of the time.

That face in the mirror — and my unsympathetic response to it — was a wakeup call for me. It forced me to see that I had to change. I had put my own needs and desires in second place for so long, I had forgotten that it was okay to put myself first in my own life. More than just okay. Imperative.

Putting ourselves first in our own lives is not selfish. It's healthy. It's actually *better* for other people when we do. We've all heard the safety instructions on airplanes. They do *not* say, "Help everyone else put on their oxygen masks, then, if you haven't passed out or died yet, put on your own."

Self-care and selfishness are two different things. The first nourishes us so we can care for others; the second nourishes nothing and cares only for itself. If we don't give ourselves time for rest, adventure, reflection, and joy, our bodies and minds end up starved for nourishment and craving attention. When that happens, we have nothing left to give. We don't *care* what anyone else's needs are. We just want them to go away. We have driven ourselves so hard, we have become selfish. Ironic, isn't it?

Robert Furey says that we can distinguish selfishness from self-care by looking at the outcome. "Feeling selfish leads to cynicism and more selfishness," he writes. "Feeling the need to care for oneself leads to recovery and rebirth."

Everyone's way of restoring and replenishing themselves is different. For me, it starts with getting enough sleep and eating three meals a day not more than six hours apart. Some days it seems impossible to do. Other days I succeed and feel so much better it's a wonder I ever allow myself to live any other way. Solid sleep and regular meals are what my body, mind, heart, and soul need to function. Period.

Beyond that, self-care for me means doing things that make me feel like myself again. Like swimming, sitting on my deck and staring at the tall pine trees, reading mysteries, browsing in bookstores, spending time in solitude, laughing with friends, spoiling my cats, listening to Vivaldi (or Talking Heads), sewing, taking ridiculously long baths, going out for a meal, getting a massage, or discovering obscure back roads. I don't always remember to do these things when I need to. I usually have to stumble again and again before I learn something.

I discovered something surprising about these self-care activities. *I don't need to spend a lot of time doing one of them before I feel better.* I was astonished to discover this.

Several years ago I was sewing a patchwork wall hanging with little rectangles of color that ran up and down the tonal scale like the notes on a xylophone. The darn thing was fabulously complicated and really easy to mess up. Normally when I am sewing a project like this, I spend three hours at a time on it. Just then, however, I didn't have hours to spare. I was on deadline for my first book. But I really, really wanted to see if the color scheme I had designed would work. So I took to nipping over to my sewing machine once a day and piecing together strips of fabric for only thirty minutes. I was amazed to discover that I would get up from my sewing feeling completely refreshed, as if I'd had a whole day with the textures, shapes, and colors I love. I have found that the same thing is true for walking and meditation. If I'm pressed for time, even a ten-minute walk or a five-minute period of sitting in silence will re-energize me.

Besides doing what feels good to us, self-care means *not* doing certain things that feel bad. For me, this includes not going to violent and sexually exploitative movies, and not spending time with mean, selfish or bigoted people.

Self-care has taught me the importance of saying no. I cannot do everything I am asked to do. What's more, I don't want to do everything I am asked to. Who would? But so often we say yes because we don't know how to say no. I don't mean that we are terminal people-pleasers. I mean that we literally don't know how. We don't know what words to use.

I sat down one day awhile back and wrote up a list called "Forty-Two Ways to Say No." It included phrases like, "That sounds interesting, but I think I'll pass," and "That doesn't work for me." (It also included "Are you out of your mind, buddy?" for those really outrageous demands on my time.) I kept this list by the phone and referred to it regularly until I didn't need a cheat sheet anymore. Interestingly, nobody laughed at my little list. Instead, they asked for copies.♥ My staff taped the list onto their desks and started saying no to me. I had to grin and bear it. My friends wanted copies. Business acquaintances wanted copies. Even several psychotherapists I know wanted copies — for their personal use. It seems that we understand how healthy it is to be able to say no, without actually being able to *say* it. But then, understanding is not the same as doing. If it

---

♥ If you want a copy, I'll email you one. (Sorry, no snail mail.) Write to SayNo@LMPress.com.

were, there wouldn't be a diet book left on the best-seller list.

Self-care requires that we learn to say no to ourselves, too. For example, on any given day I usually plan to do about four times the number of things that time will allow. I don't know if I'm perennially optimistic or just obtuse, but the result is that I end up rushing, dropping things, losing things, and stressed to the max — and I'm the one who created the stress! Sometimes for comic relief, I shout, "Who created that *meshuggeneh* schedule? Fire the bum!" Then I try to be kinder to myself the next day. I'm learning that being kind to myself means planning to do half of what I think I can get done. It also means not kicking myself when I only get through half of that. This is an ongoing practice. The fact is, it's a lot easier to say no to others who want us to do the impossible than it is to say no to the part of ourselves that thinks we can — and should — do it all.

One aspect of self-care that rarely gets addressed is being kind in the way we speak to ourselves. Author and spiritual teacher Stephen Levine says, "If we heard a couple at the next table speaking to each other the way we speak to ourselves in our mind, we wouldn't be able to eat the meal when the waiter brought it. We'd be too nauseated. But we've come to accept this self-cruelty. In fact, somehow we think it's honorable: It shows we're being good people if we put ourselves down. How merciless."♥

We all do this. We lose something and think, How stupid of me! We look in the mirror and think, You look like s——! What would our lives be like if we took a vow never to say something to ourselves that we wouldn't say to another person? My guess is that we would have a much greater ability to add love and kindness to the world. Who *wouldn't* perform better without constant criticism and name-calling?

Ignoring our own needs — because we think we don't have any or we don't want to look selfish — encourages the enemies of kindness. If I were asked what the most important chapter in this book is, I would say it's this one, "Don't Forget to Be Kind to Yourself."

That's because the door to service is the self. In fact, the door to *everything* we want to do in or for the world is the self. What else do we have to work with?

♥ From his audio tape, *Exploring Sacred Emptiness.*

Cʒ

CHAPTER 11

God's Designated Driver

What we are is God's gift to us.
What we become is our gift to God.

—LOUIS NIZER

Paloma is walking to her car in the municipal lot, a bag of Chinese herbs in one hand and an herb pot in the other. She uses the herbs to boost her immune system, which needs all the help it can get.

She has not exactly led a fairytale existence. Her firstborn son has cerebral palsy, her second son died in infancy. Then one day, when Paloma turned thirty-eight, her husband said as if joking, "I should trade you in for two nineteen-year-olds." Soon after, he moved out, went to Mexico with his girlfriend, drowned, got revived, and ended up partially paralyzed. Now Paloma's longtime lover has squamous cell cancer.

She's held up pretty well, considering. Everybody's got something, Paloma often says, her glowing smile belying the struggles she's had. Though she doesn't know it yet, she will soon be diagnosed with diabetes.

As Paloma reaches her car, she sees a young man riding a bicycle one-handed across the parking lot. His other hand holds a huge bouquet of spider mums, daisies and chrysanthemums, a joyful commotion of yellow, purple, and white. The young man rides right up to Paloma and brakes to a slightly wobbly stop.

"Would you like these flowers?" he says. "They were given to me. I have so many flowers, my house looks like a funeral parlor."

Paloma is taken aback. She hesitates, starts stammering out a word or two of polite refusal, then bursts into a smile and says, "Oh, yes, I *would* like them!"

The young man places the flowers in her arms as if she were Miss America. "Thank you for smiling," he says, then pedals away.

෪

Do you think human existence is merely the result of a random biological process involving an egg and couple of quadrillion little swimmers? Some people do, some don't. I used to think so. I was so angry at the cards I had been dealt as a kid that I used to go around quoting

Woody Allen's comment that if there is a God, he's an underachiever. Or, as a friend of mine once remarked, "Oh, I think there's a God. He just doesn't care about *me*."

I believe now that we are here for a purpose. Each of us, individually. And I believe that purpose is to add love to the world in whatever way our bodies, minds, hearts and souls tell us to. The way that's turned out to be right for me is through kindness, since kindness *is* love.

I admit that until my late thirties, I did not believe in my having a higher purpose here on earth. Nor did I have much faith that benevolent forces were running the universe. In fact, I would have sworn on a stack of Bibles that those forces didn't exist. I mean, just look around. There's enough misery, corruption, hatred, selfishness, stupidity, and sheer mean-mindedness to swamp almost anybody's good opinion of The Management. Let alone of humanity.

But something changed for me when I discovered that if I kept my eye on the small things rather than the big picture, there were indeed benevolent forces at work. I had been waiting for God to end world hunger while the real action was taking place inside my heart.

That was the moment I decided to act as if I were being guided. I confess I did not *believe* it at the time, but I decided to act as if it were true and see what happened. The results have been amazing. First of all, I am no longer constantly on the lookout for the ways in which the universe is going to frustrate my desires and thwart my plans.

Second, although acting as if I am being guided has not changed the number or intensity of difficult events in my life, it has changed *me*. It has shown me how much of my experience depends on what I do with it. I think we each create the story we are living. We can create a story about being thwarted or taken advantage of, or a story about being showered with gifts. It all depends on where we place our attention and spend our time.

Assuming I am being guided has turned out to be the best story I've ever written. It has opened my heart to the possibility that I am cared for by something greater than myself, whether I choose to call that something God or not. This shift brought with it a sense that my life has purpose and meaning, that I am not just the result of a random biological event. You could say this was merely a self-fulfilling prophecy, because believing I am here for a purpose has made me want to discover that purpose and achieve it. But so what? However it worked, it *worked*.

I think we are all here for the same purpose, though how we achieve that purpose depends on our unique interests and abilities. I think our purpose is to be God's designated driver. God doesn't have hands. God can't do everything that needs to be done in our world. God depends on us.

There's an old story about a man disappointed in the Almighty. He climbs a mountain so God can hear him and starts chewing out the Supreme Being. "Things are a mess down here! We fight all the time! The rich eat lamb while the poor eat dirt! The winter is coming and we cannot afford warm shoes. How can you let us suffer? Why don't you send someone to help us?"

The heavens open and God leans down. "I did send someone," God intones. "I sent you."

This is why kindness is — and isn't — about us. Kindness is about us because we are the ones responsible for taking kind action. But it's also not about us because kindness is Spirit acting through us. It's God using our hands to help the world because God doesn't have any. One of the reasons kindness makes us so powerful is that we are acting like God's hands. When we are kind, the power of Spirit inhabits and moves through us.

Peter Reinhart, in his book *Bread Upon the Waters*, says each of us has the ability to be "a channel for grace." Spiritual teacher Gay Luce describes wanting to be "a tuning fork for the divine." I love that image: Life gives us a thwack to activate us, and we (no doubt after saying "Ouch!!") vibrate with Divine Love, which travels out into the world to the ears that most need to hear it.

Being kind to someone not only channels grace to them, it honors the grace *in* them. When I studied yoga, we were taught to bow to each other at the end of class and say, "Namaste." Our yoga teacher, an elegant Western woman in her early seventies, explained that "namaste" means, "All that is God in me bows to all that is God in you." I have heard other translations of the word over the years, but none that felt so right.

Recognizing God in another person may seem like a daunting task. Susan Trott puts it much more simply. The message of her wonderful little book, *The Holy Man*, is: Treat everyone you meet as holy.

To me, kindness is the divine use of personal power, the giving of grace to another. In doing so, we ourselves are graced. The gifts we have been given (health, creativity, financial stability, contentment, tenacity — whatever they may be) were given so we could pass them along to others. The wisdom traditions hold that the only way to keep our gifts intact *is* to pass them on. If we try to keep them to ourselves, they dry up. As Lewis Hyde puts it in *The Gift*, "In the world of gift...you not only can have your cake and eat it too, you can't have your cake *unless* you eat it."

The distinguished Quaker author Parker Palmer concurs and goes one step further. "If you receive a gift, you keep it alive not by clinging to it but by passing it along," he writes. "The true law of life is that we generate more of whatever seems scarce by trusting its supply and passing it around."♥

Many years ago, a grateful student asked author Robert Heinlein if there was something she could do to thank him. "Your books have done so much for me," she

---

♥ From *Let Your Life Speak: Listening for the Voice of Vocation*. I wish everyone could read this small book, whether they are searching for their calling or not. It is wise, authentic, and beautifully written. I admire Parker Palmer immensely.

said. "I want to give something back." Heinlein shook his head gently and told her, "You don't give back, you give forward."♥♥

I think that every act of kindness is an act of giving forward. I use "giving forward" here to mean both giving to the one in front of us and giving toward the future, toward progress, toward what is higher, greater, more worthy of our time, attention, and energy. One act of kindness sets the ball rolling for the next. And the next and the next. It's like a reverse Domino Theory, where each domino is lifted by the one behind it until every piece is standing tall.

♥♥ This is the also theme of Catherine Ryan Hyde's novel *Pay It Forward*. The movie got mixed reviews, but I thought the book was outstanding.

A SHORT COURSE IN KINDNESS

ଔ

CHAPTER 12

Strategies and Tactics

for the Kindness Revolution

The only way to ensure that
kindness lives on your planet
is to put it there yourself.

—ROBERT J. FUREY, *THE JOY OF KINDNESS*

Have the stories of kindness I've shared in this book seemed extraordinary? The fact is, they are and they aren't. They *are* remarkable stories, but they are not extraordinary — that is, they are not out of the ordinary.

I didn't contact hundreds of people asking for their experiences of kindness. I asked ten specific people. Nine responded, some with more than one story. Altogether, I gathered thirteen stories of kindness. Nine of these stories you have already read, and you can judge for yourself how powerful they are.

I think there is so much more kindness at work in our world than we are aware of. In a way, we need to bring kindness out of the closet. People like me, who don't mind being considered hopelessly naïve or unhip, need some company out here trying to turn Reality-TV Land into Kindness Country. I hope you'll join me.

Stories of unkindness make the headlines, get chewed over on talk radio, get passed by word of mouth. Dear old kindness, however, isn't getting the P.R. it deserves! It's not considered news (unless it involves a gorilla), and it doesn't lend itself to headlines or sound bites. Kindness is subtle. It's about love, connection, and small acts that make a world of difference in someone's life. Sometimes it's even hard to explain why a specific act of kindness has such a big impact. Take the woman who made a free ham and provolone on rye for someone who was bone tired from visiting her mom in the nursing home. Can you imagine your favorite news anchor announcing, "Coming up, a deli angel donates dinner! Stay tuned."

That's why spreading stories of kindness is up to us. It's also the first of the two strategies that together will spread kindness across the world.

Remember the miracle of connection that took place on that bus in Chicago? It would not have happened if one of the passengers hadn't shared with his fellow riders the story of the gorilla that saved the toddler. Look at what happened. This man reads the story of the gorilla's actions aloud. This starts a second story of kindness: The people on the bus laugh and smile and talk to each other. Tovah is moved to offer her seat to someone who needs it, something she's *never* done before. When she tells her class the story a few months later, Tovah's English teacher is affected by it. Then the teacher asks Tovah to tell the story to a visiting author. It affects the author, Vivian Gussin Paley, who puts it in her book, *The Kindness of Children*. That's in 1999, three years after the event. Three more years go by and I read the story in Paley's book. It affects me. I share the story with you. Talk about stories spreading!

Don't forget, we're *not* talking about the story of the gorilla, which we would expect to have a long shelf life. We are talking about the story of people on a bus who hear the story of the gorilla, feel good, and immediately change the way they treat each other.

The tactics for this first strategy, spreading kindness through storytelling, are straightforward. When someone is kind to us, we tell people about it. We ask others about kindness they have given and received. We become kindness talent-spotters by developing our ability to recognize kindness wherever it occurs and in whatever form it takes. We help kids do the same thing. This is especially important. Kids need to be reminded as much as we do — maybe more — that good things can happen in the real world.

The second strategy for spreading kindness is to *be* kind. The tactics for achieving this strategy are many, and I will share some of them with you in a moment. Before I do, though, I want to stress that *you* are the best source of ideas for being kind. Being kind is an incredibly creative act. That's part of why it feels so good. When you notice an opening for kindness, notice too your first impulse about what to do. No matter what you may read in my list of tactics, follow your instincts about what is best in the situation. And when in doubt, lead with your heart.

The Ten Tactics

♥ **Small acts can have big effects.** No kind act is too small if it comes from the heart. I discovered this recently when I bought a house and put an ad in the paper to rent the apartment over the garage. The first day I had eight calls. The second day I had thirteen calls. The third day I had twenty-four calls. And so on. The phone was driving me nuts! Finally, I just let my answering machine pick up.

A few days later, when the total of calls had reached sixty-three and I had found a wonderful tenant, I sat down and called back the people whom I hadn't spoken to personally. After delivering the bad news, I found myself adding, "Good luck with your house hunt. I know it's tough." I hadn't been planning to say that. It just popped out because I'd been a renter all my life and I knew how hard — and scary — it can be to find a place to live.

A small thing, but the response was huge. I could feel the gratitude at the other end of the line. Gratitude that someone understood how hard it was to find a home, that someone was treating them as if they mattered. I had had no idea that my saying those few words would mean so much.

♥ **Be guided by the Better-Than-Golden Rule.** This "rule" asks not that we do unto others as we would have them do unto us, but that we do unto others as *they would have us* do unto them. To be genuinely helpful, we need to give people the help they need, not the help we think they need. I had a lesson in this awhile back when I got an unexpected check and used part of it to buy some warm clothes for a friend in the Midwest. Winter was about to descend and I knew she was strapped for cash. She thanked me for the clothes and said they looked great. I was very pleased.

A couple of months later, I found out that what she had needed more than warm clothing was a new desk chair so she could work at her computer without her back hurting. But I hadn't asked. I had given her what I would have wanted in her place.

♥ **Listen, listen, listen (and occasionally ask questions).** Have you ever been lucky enough to have a friend who could really listen to you? Just listen? Not try to fix what is bothering you, not judge you, and not offer their opinion, tell you about a similar experience they had, or say "I know what you mean." Friends like that are worth twice their weight in rubies. We can be that friend, to our friends as well as to our family, colleagues, acquaintances, strangers — to anyone who needs to talk and be heard. We can listen to them with an open heart and a gentle gaze, occasionally nodding, perhaps asking a question or two, and never once consulting our watch. This simple act can make an incalculable difference to someone.

♥ **Accept the kindness of others.** This is more important than you may think. Kindness refused stops the flow of kindness. It's related to the teaching about keeping our gifts alive by passing them on to others. If someone passes a gift to us, we need to receive it with gratitude, not turn away from it saying, "Oh, no, you mustn't." It may take some practice, but the proper response to an act of kindness is simply, "Thank you." How can we expect others to accept our kindness if we refuse to accept theirs?

♥ **Talk about the hard stuff.** When I ran my un-profit♥ organization for people healing from childhood

---

♥ As distinguished from a non-profit organization, which, though operating with the same idealistic motives, has the blessing of the abuse, I saw with complete clarity what a kindness it is to share our dark experiences with others. I have talked before audiences of five and audiences of three hundred about being molested and its aftereffects, such as depression, shame, addiction, and spiritual emptiness. I was never sorry I did. At each event I heard a collective sigh of relief that someone was telling the truth about what many in the audience had kept secret for so long.

Yes, it is a risk to offer one's private story to strangers, but having the courage to take risks is part of what it takes to be kind. Sometimes people need to hear that others have suffered hardships and survived them. As long as the situation is appropriate (not a business meeting or a bridal shower), we can do untold good by having the kindness to share the dark side of our lives. Especially with young people.

A friend of mine in her fifties, Robin, shared her story of being sexually abused as a child with her niece, who is thirteen. Five months later, the niece's best friend asked to talk with Robin. It turned out that the girl had been raped by her stepfather. She had told her mother and the stepfather had moved out of the family home. The girl was in counseling, too. But she needed to talk to someone who had been there — and who had come out on the other side of

---

IRS and may actually be able to pay its bills. Don't try looking for this word in the dictionary. I made it up.

the dark times. Robin talked with the girl and told her she could call any time. A week or so later, the girl phoned with a question.

"The one word I want to ask you about is...." She hesitated. "What do you think about kindness? Is it worth being kind in such a horrible world?"

Robin told her that yes, it was.

Who else but someone who had been hurt just as cruelly could have answered the teenager's question this way and been believed? It is for young people like this that we need to be open about the painful parts of our lives.

♥ **When action is called for, act.** This is what it comes down to. All that precedes this moment is essential — empathy, choice, sense of self, and courage — but without action, none of that matters. Intentions aren't enough when it comes to kindness. We need to step forward and take action — tap on the car window of the woman who's crying, sit at a cafeteria table and offer help to a stranger, take the lost wallet away from the person rifling through it, or recite sonnets in the operating theater under the eyes of our no-nonsense colleagues. Our willingness to interrupt the normal course of our lives and take action is a big piece of the message that our kind act conveys. It says, I care enough about what is happening to you to stop what I am doing and turn my attention to your situation.

♥ **Offer companionship in whatever form it is needed.**
Parker Palmer, the Quaker author, tells about two
periods in his forties when he sank into deep
depression. Some of the people who came to see how
he was doing suggested he go outside in the sunshine
because that would surely make him feel better. Their
advice only made him feel worse. Others reminded
him of what a good person he was, how many people
he had helped with teachings, and thought this would
cheer him up. Palmer thought, I sure fooled them.
Still others told him they knew exactly how he felt.
He thought, No you don't.

Then one day a friend named Bill stopped in. He
asked Palmer if he could massage his feet. Palmer,
surprised, said okay. Every afternoon after that, Bill
stopped by, removed Palmer's socks, and gently
massaged his feet for half an hour. Nothing more,
nothing less. It was the only kind of human contact
that Palmer was able to *feel*. It helped in ways Palmer
says he cannot fully articulate to this day.

Bill offered his kindness and companionship in
the only form he thought Palmer could stand: touch.
He looked at the situation and offered what he
thought was needed, no matter the unorthodox form
it took. His friend's response confirmed that he'd
guessed right.

♥ **Encourage laughter.** When I was eight, I had a friend
named Christine. Her mom, Françoise, was French
and she was my mom's best friend. Christine's dad

was Spanish and I hardly ever saw him when I went over to play. One evening, my mother came to my room and said, "Christine's father was in the hospital, and he died tonight. I am going to see Françoise. Do you want to come?"

I remember arriving at their apartment, which was over a small grocery store. We climbed the steep wooden stairs. Françoise opened the door. She was sobbing. She threw her arms around my mother and wailed. I had never seen a grownup cry like that before. My mom and Françoise took a bottle and glasses and went up to the third floor to talk while Christine and I played in her room. When they came down a while later, I was amazed to see Françoise was laughing.

In the car on the way home, I asked, "Mom, why was Françoise laughing? Her husband just died." My mother said, "Honey, she's laughing now, but she'll be crying again soon."

I understand now what my mother was doing for her friend: She was giving her a momentary break from her terrible grief. Laughter can be a gift of great kindness.

It also feels good! When we're around kindness — whether we are offering it, receiving it, or witnessing it — it can tickle us, make us laugh out loud with surprise and joy, like those testy commuters riding the bus in Chicago. We feel better about ourselves and the world. Hmm. Wouldn't it be interesting if the "feel good" generation took up kindness as its stimulant of choice?

♥ **Be encouraging.** Kindness is having faith in another person's ability to achieve their goal when they don't have faith in themselves. Those inner voices of ours that say, "You'll never make it. What made you think you could pull that off?" need to be countered by voices that say with complete confidence, "I know you can do it. I believe in you. Don't give up. You're almost there. I'm behind you all the way." Wouldn't it feel good to hear those words when you are struggling to do something hard? It would to me. That's why I say them to other people when they seem to be losing sight of their dreams.

♥ **Be kind to yourself.** I have put this tactic last, but not because it is of least importance. Frankly, it's probably the most important tactic of all. It is the axis on which all other tactics turn. If we can respect and care for our own needs, we can respect and care for the needs of others. If we care for others but not ourselves, it's only a matter of time before we stop caring for others. As Robert Furey puts it, "You have to protect your ability to give. If not, you may give out."

Try giving yourself a week in which you carry out your normal life *and* pay attention daily to your needs for rest, nourishment, sleep, play, solitude, exercise, creativity — whatever it is that renews and replenishes you. (Remember, you don't have to spend huge chunks of time on self-care — except for sleeping, of course — in order to feel the benefit.) If you try this, I think you will see such a difference in your ability to empathize with and take action in the service of others, you will be astonished. But you won't find out if you don't give it a try.

I have no doubt that we *can* start a Kindness Revolution. Strategies and tactics like these, along with the ones you devise for yourself, will set change in motion. Contagion will do its part. The other forces in the universe, which would really rather we didn't blow up all God's lovely creations in one big fit of temper, will help us. I cannot tell you for certain what the outcome will be, but I can tell you what I've got in mind.

Someone I don't know well asked me the other day what I was planning to do with the rest of my life.

"Change the world," I replied.

There was a pause. Then she asked, "What part?"

"All of it," I said.

ଔ

CHAPTER 13

Changing the World

Nothing can stop an idea whose time has come.

—JOHANN WOLFGANG VON GOETHE

I T is the early 1950s. I am a little girl growing up outside Philadelphia, where history is a powerful presence. My mother, father, older brother, and I live in an 18th century farmer's house, a double house knocked into one when my parents bought it in 1953. At the foot of the long hill behind the house runs a wide creek — full of crayfish and deep enough to canoe in — that feeds a broad, short waterfall, which once powered a grist mill. The remains of the mill, a seven-foot fieldstone pillar topped by the huge round millstone against which grain was once been crushed, sits in mid-creek at the foot of the falls. Beyond the creek, reached by a wooden bridge, are acres and acres of tangled woodland, paradise for a child.

Although I am only four, I badly need a paradise. Paradise is where my once-adored grandfather with his ticklish, brushy mustache can't guide my small hand over his penis while he says confusing things to me. Paradise is where I don't have to go to nursery school and join the circle of adults in the basement, who touch me and the other "special" children, who turn on blinding lights and take movies of us naked. Finally, paradise is where my own father, the yearning, dark-browed second son of the family, does not shuffle softly into my bedroom at night, year after year, pleading silently for love from someone who will never ask anything of him — and who will join him in pretending it never happened.

The nine years of sexual abuse I suffered as a child leave a deep wound in me, like a black hole in my heart, that will pursue me first into young adulthood and then into middle age. It will take twelve years of psychotherapy, seven years of meditation, five kinds of antidepressants (though not all at once), and the love and kindness of countless friends, mentors, and professionals before my body, mind, heart, and spirit are healed.

When I finally emerge from my cocoon of healing, softer now and more fully aware, I rejoin the world and find myself seeing it with new eyes. Looking around me at this strange new place, I am struck by how precious life is and how lucky I am to be living it. That which I would have tossed away like a spent match before, I now see as holy.

Even the simplest things, like a garage sale with strangers crowding eagerly around my outlived possessions, or a trip into town to buy a loaf of fresh-baked bread, seem charged with an inner light. Tears, once so near the surface from the pain I carried, now well up in unexpected moments of gladness and gratitude.

One day I realize I have fallen in love with the world — *this* world, with its tornadoes, polluted beaches, child molesters, thieves, taxes, invading armies, liars, cheaters, and know-it-alls. This world. Exactly the way it is.

I had wanted to love only the good stuff, to close my heart to the bad things in life, but all that did was leave me with a closed heart. I see that if I let people who make wars, drive up prices, and steal food from the hungry win, if I respond to them by closing my heart, I am the one who gets short-changed. I am the one who walks around with a lump of lead in her chest instead of kindness, mercy, compassion and joy.

By keeping my heart open, I feel myself coming into my true personal power — the power of a kind heart with the courage to act on its beliefs. People who have known me a long time might tell you I have always been kind. Maybe. More likely I was just being nice and it looked like kind to them. I do know I have always been a fierce protector of the weak and unjustly accused. And I have always been determined to change the world. You can imagine why.

 C8

My intention in writing this book is to change the world. I used to apologize for believing I could do this. I don't anymore. Our dear, lush, confounding world needs changing desperately, and if no one has the nerve to stand up and say they're willing to try, what will happen to us?

Change is the very nature of life. Everything changes, the good stuff and the bad. So the only substantive argument that my desire to change the world is hare-brained is the size of my target. The whole world?

Sure. Because the way you change the world — the *only* way you change the world — is one heart at a time. You start with yourself, then see what happens. In the end you discover two things:

1. One person is a lot
2. Change, like kindness, is contagious

Despite the frontier spirit in our blood, I think we underestimate the power of the individual. Each of us holds the world in the palm of our hand. We have the power to create or destroy. To bring happiness or pain. Moment by moment. Everything happens in the moment. The big picture is nothing more than a million moments all strung together. When we stop to offer kindness to someone, we have an impact on the big picture because we are having an impact on the immediate moment. We need only think of Tovah's story to remind ourselves how far-reaching a single act of kindness can be.

This ability to create change is what's so wonderful about our lives. We are not riding a train that is driven by someone else. We are the train. We are even the tracks. We can choose our destination. We can create the future by the way we act. Right now. Is unkindness winning? We can change that! We don't need new laws or special equipment. You and I can do it with our kind words and actions.

I believe that love — which is the stuff kindness is made of — will prevail. It is infinitely more powerful than hate. I have seen this in my own life. Experiencing great harm at the hands of the people I looked to for love should have made my heart shrink, wither, and close up tight. Yet, as I discovered when I faced the truth of what happened to me and healed it, I have love to spare. I have kindness to spare. It's as if I have somehow expanded to encompass those terrible events. As if I were the ocean and the abuse a single drop of poison in a billion gallons of shining blue water.

My past has taught me well the importance of love and the relative unimportance of just about everything else. Through love we find energy, contentment, and wisdom greater than we'd ever dreamed. Without love, the glittering prizes of our modern lives sooner or later turn to dust.

That is why kindness is a revolution whose time has come. We deserve to see what the world looks like when kind people are running our corporations and sitting in Congress. We deserve to see how our culture changes when kind people are in charge of publishing our newspapers, hosting newscasts, producing movies, and designing video games.

And — most important of all — we deserve to see what our future looks like when only kind people are allowed to educate our children.

We can change the world because we *are* the world. You and I and your kids and your neighbors and the guy jogging past you at dawn and the woman riding the elevator down with you after a long day's work.

We know the tide of unkindness won't be easily turned. So what? I'm backing the Kindness Revolution.

And I need you with me.

CHANGING THE WORLD

A SHORT COURSE IN KINDNESS

Now Tell Me Your Stories

There is nothing that spreads kindness faster than sharing our stories of the moments in our lives when we have given, received, or witnessed an act of kindness.

These acts are often small ones, done without fanfare. Yet they touch us, warm our hearts, and weave themselves subtly into the fabric of our lives. They give us hope in the midst of despair.

Let's make the commitment to share these stories with each other. Send me your stories of simple acts of human kindness. Be sure to include a return address or phone number where I can reach you if I need to. In turn, I will share your stories with the audiences I speak to and in my future books.

Together, we will spread the word that kindness is alive and well on our precious planet.

Send your stories to:

- ♥ Margot@MargotSilkForrest.com

- ♥ Margot Silk Forrest
  c/o L.M. Press
  P.O. Box 345
  Cayucos, CA 93430

Index

Acknowledgements

No woman is an island, especially when she's writing a book. My deepest thanks go to the family members, friends, and colleagues who offered me their love, stories, ideas, encouragement, patience, professional advice, and support. Among them are:

My mother, Patricia Delaney, who taught me the incomparable value of love, freedom, and kindness;

Holly A. Gibson, Molly Fisk, Susan Borkin, Kathy Duguid, Yvonne Rand, Andy Ryan, Nancy Roberts, Rachel Park, Jenna Kinghorn, Margaret Lindquist, Linda Brady, and Nancy Marie, who helped with the ideas and the writing in this book;

Kate Paddock and S. Beverley Spencer, whose artistic skills and cover design make this book a joy to look at;

Catherine Ryan Hyde, who graciously took time from working on her new novel to write the inspiring foreword;

Yvonne Rand, Suey Irvine, Kathy Simmons, Holly A. Gibson, Nadine Anderberg, Anita Montero, and Lisa Derr (whose first novel, *A Song Between Lives*, is now available from www.xlibris.com), who shared their stories of kindness;

And Ellen Bass, Laura Davis, Kathleen DesMaisons, Bob Kriegel, Peter Reinhart, Rayona Sharpnack, and Barbara Waugh, who so warmly welcomed this book's arrival in the world.

Give the Gift of
kindness

To get extra copies of A SHORT COURSE IN KINDNESS:

- ♥ Go to your favorite local bookstore
- ♥ Order via our web site, www.LMPress.com
- ♥ Call us with your order at (805) 545-0888
- ♥ Fax your order to us at (805) 435-1472
- ♥ Mail your order to us at L. M. Press, P.O. Box 345, Cayucos, CA 93430

NAME_____

STREET ADDRESS_____

CITY, STATE, AND ZIP_____

DAYTIME PHONE_____

EMAIL ADDRESS _____

QUANTITY	TITLE	EACH	TOTAL
_____	A SHORT COURSE IN KINDNESS	$ 12.00	_____

SHIPPING: $3 FOR 1ST BOOK, $1.25 FOR EACH ADDITIONAL _____

CA. RESIDENTS ADD 7.25% TAX _____

___ VISA/MASTERCARD OR   TOTAL DUE _____

___ CHECK/ MONEY ORDER ENCLOSED

CARD NUMBER _____ EXP DATE _____

SIGNATURE_____

☐ **To request a copy signed by the author, please check this box AND order directly from L.M. Press**